Pop Up (AR)t
A Technology Enhanced Publication

Important information for purchasers & readers:

This book presents virtual three-dimensional artwork by eighteen artists exploring varying aspects of what that means – technically, conceptually, and artistically.

To take advantage of the enhanced experience presented in this volume requires the use of a software application running on your smart phone or tablet operating under iOS or Android.

The app, Wikitude, is available at the Apple App Store or through Google Play, and is a free download. In the App, search for CoCA Pop Up (AR)t Book to view the 3D artwork by pointing your device's camera at the square image in the upper right corner of each right hand page.

For further information, see The Software on page 11.

I0494560

CENTER ON CONTEMPORARY ART

Center on Contemporary Art

Published May 2016 by:
Center on Contemporary Art
7601 Greenwood Avenue North,
Suite 108
Seattle, Washington 98103

http://www.cocaseattle.org
info@cocaseattle.org
206 728-1980

Copyright ©2016
Center on Contemporary Art
ISBN: 978-0-9909838-6-6

Producer:
Ray C. Freeman III

Jurors:
David Francis
Joseph Roberts

Cover art:
Stephen Rock

Artists' images and texts used by permission. All rights reserved. No part of this book may be reproduced in any manner whatsoever without written permission except in the case of brief quotations embodied in critical articles and reviews

Funders:
4Culture
Seattle Foundation
Individual Donors
CoCA Members
Office of Arts and Cultural Affairs

Board of Directors:
Miguel Edwards, President
Sara Everett, Vice President
Tina Gonsalves, Chair
Lorrie Cardoso, Vice Chair
Dan Hawkins, Treasurer
Talia Silveri Wright, Secretary
Joseph Bisacca, Director
Kalindi Kunis, Director
Todd Lawson, Director
Travis Monroe, Director
Michele Osgood, Director
Joseph Roberts, Director, Curator
David Ruggiero, Treasurer
Jackie Shultz, Director
Kate Vrijmoet, Director

Board of Advisors:
Ray C. Freeman III, Publisher
David Francis, PhD, Curator at Large

CoCA Staff:
Nichole DeMent, Executive Director
Caroline Parry, Administrative & Program Associate

Anna R Hurwitz, Director, CoCA Archives Project

Jennifer Cha, Kacey Lewis, Alex Robinson,
Katja Schatte, Interns

Sponsors:
Good Arts LLC
Rock's Studio
Rubix Apartments
Elysian Brewing
Robert E Frey / Lakeside Advisors
Castanes Architects, P. S., A.I.A.

Contents

Introduction
Ray C. Freeman III, Producer

I have been waiting for this day for a long time. The publication of 3D models is a problem that has dogged me for years. A 3D model is a thing, and as Magritte taught us, a picture of a thing is not the thing.

In 1989, Generic Software introduced a product they called 3D Drafting, or 3DD for short. I had been first a product tester of Generic CADD, then author of the user documentation, then a power user, the author of two books on the program, and finally a columnist for the Generic News. In these various roles, I had used their 2D CADD product to produce numerous drawings for publication, including many 3D drawings created using conventional drafting techniques, including isometrics, axonometrics, and perspectives, applied to computer drafting. By the time 3DD appeared, in fact, I had published a program for converting 2D Generic CADD drawings into perspective views.

All of these drawings, no matter the projection technique however, had something in common, They were essentially frozen 2D views of a 3D object, building, or scene, i.e. a picture of the thing. Not the thing itself. One could not turn the drawing around and see it from the other side. That required another drawing. V ery importantly, it was the creator of the drawing who controlled the point of view, not the consumer of the drawing. If I wanted to highlight something by putting it front and center in the drawing, I could do that. Conversely, if I wanted to hide it behind a column, I could do that, too.

Back in the day, there was a great deal of hand-wringing over which conveyed the most (and best) information, parallel-line or perspective projections, both flattened 2D representations of three dimensions. Perspective can be seen as a more visual, experientially-based construct, while the axonometric represents a more detached intellectually based point of view from which the viewer can derive more specific information. It is explanatory in nature, rather than illustrative. On the other side of the coin, the perspective format is limited as an analytical tool by the assumption of a particular point of view , while the axonometric can be less useful for establishing exactly what something looks like. Articles were written, lectures were given, and commentary was written about the lectures. But I digress.

As an early tester of Generic 3D, and as the author of the documentation, I had the opportuniy to create numerous models using the software. When designing (and I did in fact use the program for design, not just drafting), I often worked in various isometric views, as these could be obtained from any angle, but presented my drawings to my clients as perspectives. The illustrations on the following page are among those early drawings, for a store fixture I designed for the Zebra Club in Seattle. The isometric represents how I saw it on the screen, and the perspective is an example of how I showed it to the client. Although I wasn't keen on it at the time, the word "Drafting" in the name of the product was oddly accurate, because although the user worked in 3D, the end result was usually a 2D drawing representing the 3D model.

When the program was released, I was approached by the editor of the Generic News about using some of my models as examples in their story about the new product. Among other drawings, I sent my model of the store fixture to the editor, and waited with bated breath for the next issue to arrive in the mail.

When it did, I was aghast! Much to my chagrin, the model had been rendered in orthographic projection, a view I had never seen before. Not only that, but there was a credit next to it that stated "drawing by Ray C. Freeman III". In point of fact, I did not make that drawing. I made the model from which it was generated. I was not particularly happy with the drawing, which was not only

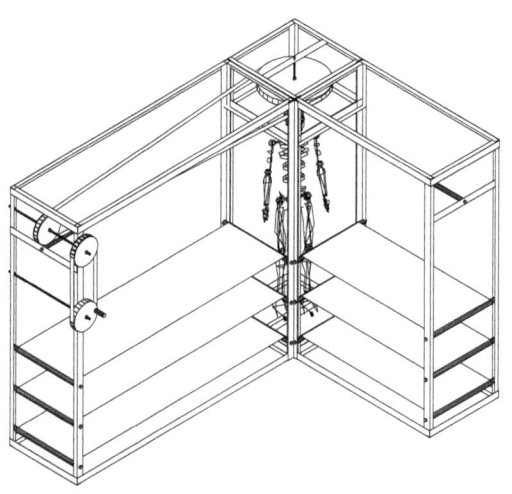

Three views of the same model, circa 1989

Isometric

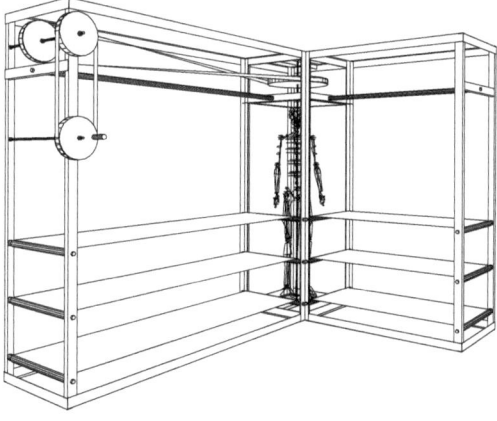

Perspective

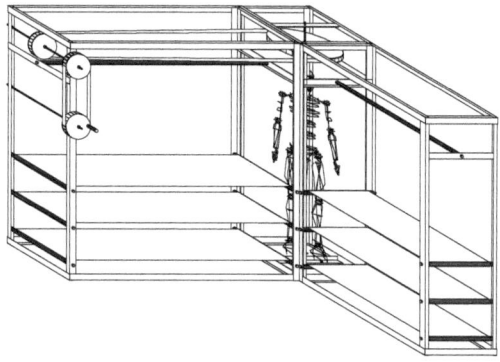

Orthographic

not a very good example of what the software could do, but unflattering to the design as well.

A very important lesson had been learned. You can't print a model. You can only print a drawing. The drawing is a physical representation of the model, which is in turn a virtual representation of a physical thing. T alk about threachery – it's twice removed! Over the years, I have had many 3D drawings published, in the Generic News and elsewhere, but I have made it a point to never send a model. I have always generated the drawing that was to be printed myself.

Fortunately, more recent technological innovations have changed the landscape, to some extent. It is now possible for the viewer to have more direct access to the model itself, or at least the vantage point from which it is viewed. Almost every automobile manufacturer's website features interactive 3D views of their latest offerings, where you can spin the car around and see it from all sides. Realtors offer much the same for their high-end homes.

I can send a digital model to you, and if you have a 3D printer, you can print it and hold a small representation of the actual object in your hand. Software and hardware offerings from Cardboard VR to Oculus Rift allow you to see a virtual environment through goggles or a head mounted display simply by looking around.

Several years ago, while serving as a reviewer for Dace Campbell's Master's thesis in the Machine Design Group at the University of Washington, I was introduced to the idea of Augmented Reality, which Dace had explored as part of his thesis, and I have pursued it as an interest ever since. At first, access to the technology was limited. I had to write my own software just to experiment with it, but even these crude results were promising. In due time of course, apps began appearing for iOS and elsewhere. Eventually a tool appeared that allowed you to create your own applications and publish your own AR models. Augmented Reality was now accessible to the general public and - more importantly - to artists.

For this publication, I have broken my own rule and asked artists to send models, not drawings. I asked them to take a leap of faith that I would do my best to see that their artistic intent would not suffer egregiously in the publication effort. However, the target software has limitations, and the conversion of the models from their original formats, with artists working on a variety of software and hardware platforms is not perfect. What is presented is the best that we could achieve with the technology at hand, in a reasonable time frame.

However, if we wait, we will have to start over again. Technology is changing as I write this. Augmented Reality is a moving target, gaining steam by the minute. Currently Augmented Reality can be considered the addition of information (i.e. augmentation) to a real-time camera view of reality. This can be additional visual information, as in "stuff that isn't really there", or access to contextual data, triggered by either visual markers in the camera's view, GPS data related to the camera's location and orientation, or other real-world indicators.

In our case, the "reality" is this book. We are presenting information in the form of imagery and text, together with a "target" image, over which the model, or "augmented" part of the content is displayed. You can hold the book in your hand or set it on the table in front of you, view the target image through your handheld device, and as you turn the book (or yourself), control the viewpoint from which you see the three dimensional artwork, as the software tracks the location and orientation of the target and adjusts the view of the model accordingly.

This limited use of Augmented Reality barely scratches the surface. Since this project was conceived, even the

software that we are using has added the capability of using a scene in the real world as a target "image". This allows the artist to add three dimensional elements into a real time camera view of the real world, not just a static image. Animated models, as well, are now possible.

But you have to start somewhere. It was my goal to get this technology in front of artists and see what they would do. Some of the artists were already working in 3D, and have migrated their existing work to this new platform. Others have created digital counterparts to existing or proposed real world sculptures. Still others are working in 3D for the first time, bringing their artistic sensibilities more directly to bear, without an intervening step.

Some have used expensive professional tools to create their models, and others have used free, open-source, or shareware products. While the variation in tools certainly plays a role, I hope that it is more the diversity of artistic intent that shines through as you peruse this volume. One of the curatorial goals was to present a wide variety of approaches, hoping to include divergent subject matter, techniques, and intent, and to explore, within the limitations of a book, a wide variety of artistic and experimental uses of the technology.

As one would expect with an emerging technology, the level of integration between the target image and the model itself varies from artwork to artwork. In some instances, such as L. Kelly Lyles' "Zagnut" and Stephen Rock's "Between Beauty & Chaos", and to some extent Karen Hackenberg's "American Sea Urchin II", the final artwork is a composite of the two. In other cases, the 2D target is a version or view of the 3D model itself, while still others use the target as a reference image or icon of the artwork, not related physically, but conceptually. The pit balls of Corey Dunlap's image, or the moon in Alan Fulle's come to mind. This relationship between the printed page and the 3D model is one of the things that

I hoped to see explored in these projects, and it's a testament to the creativity of these artists that a variety of approaches are represented.

As with any mode of representation, there is the question of scale to deal with, as well. The more conceptual and abstract pieces have no real scale, so what you see is what you get. In other cases, entire buildings are represented in the space allowable on these pages, and on the screen of the device through which you are viewing the artwork. Similarly, the level of detail is limited by these same constraints.

On the other hand, this book in many ways emulates the traditional pop-up book, which has even more constraints. Still, great masterpieces in paper art and engineering have been created using that form factor, and I hope that by publishing this volume, we are adding to an understanding of the media, illustrating some of what can be done, and encouraging others to give it a go.

I would like to thank CoCA for letting me pursue this, the jurors for their input and advice, and the artists for working with me over the past several months to convert, cajole, and squeeze thier models into this format. Many models had to be rebuilt, modified, or otherwise adjusted to work with our chosen technology, and you have all been very forgiving.

In the interest of full disclosure, I should point out that I have, to some extent, intervened in every artwork in this book, for better or worse. In some cases, as with Miguel Edwards, Alan Fulle, Karen Hackenberg, and Joseph Reyes, I built the model myself from the artists's sketches and/or photos. With others, modifications were required. I rebuilt many of the objects in Corey Dunlap's model in order to reduce the polygon count. The landscape below Amiko Matsuo's model was cropped to the square format and to make the main model larger . Megan

Geckler's model was rebuilt to work with the software, and replicated upwards according to her instructions. BK Tran's and Casey Scalf's models didn't survive the conversion from SketchUp, so the colors and patterns needed to be re-applied. Reilly Donovan, Nina McGowan, Jeff Mihalyo, and Bradley Tsalyuk all worked with me to get their models across the digital divide intact. At the far end of the spectrum, j shagam developed custom software to explore an idea and deliver a model, and Xavier Lopez Jr. gave me some conceptual guidance, but otherwise left me free to interpret his work in this format.

Of course, I take responsibility for any degradation, incompleteness, or other damage done to these beautiful artworks in the process. One of the advantages of the mechanism by which we have published this book is that the virtual content can be upgraded even after printing. If any of the artists, for example, aren't happy with the results, they can be revisited, and you may see these models improve upon a second, third, or hundredth viewing.

Although I anticipate only minor changes in these models to correct errors, improve lighting, and clear up any other miscommunications after the fact, it would be interesting to explore this aspect of the technology as an integral concept in either an individual artwork or an entire volume. Art that changes every time you look at it. A book that is new again every time you pick it up. Maybe I won't have to wait so long for that.

Ray is an award-winning architect who has practiced in Seattle for more than 30 years, both through his former firm, WORKSHOP 3D Design Studio, and through collaborations with others. He was the founder of CyberToys, Inc., where he produced multi-media software for LEGO and the White House, and was President of Blueprint: for Architecture 1984-1985. He has served as Curator, Treasure, and President of the Board for CoCA, and is currently an advisor, in the role of Publisher.

For Optimum Results
David Francis, Juror

The development of perspective since the Renaissance, as David Hockney's *Secret Knowledge* (2006) wonderfully points out, can be understood technologically as well as aesthetically, since (as the Hockney-Falco thesis argues), it seems highly likely that an array of lenses, instruments, and other paraphernalia helped facilitate this leap in representation. To skip ahead and offer an executive summary of my own little take in the first paragraph: the question of whether it is art or not, while possibly interesting in various critical contexts, is superseded by the almost palpable sense that aside from such taxonomic questions, the resulting experiments open new spaces for inquiry, for how perception works in this particular sub-system of newly emerged, representational reality. (A related question might be, given that holodeck–integrated reality exists, *how do we make art in that space?* Whether we realize it or not, we are in fact already exploring such a praxis.)

Back to instruments and devices: later innovations like the Claude glass and, by another leap, the Aeolian harp and even the camera itself, add to the evidence that our ongoing exploration and understanding of representing objects in space (especially and traditionally in painting but broadly transferable) is often connected to the development of new technological interfaces that create relatively *untested* environments for representational portrayal. Interestingly, these devices are often not publically identified, remaining proprietary, concealed from the customer who buys only the end result (traditionally speaking, at least in terms of the commodity -object of art). (Venetian glass maestros thus kept technological secrets very closely for 1,000 years.)

Now, as contemporary art expands to encompass social practice, new media, conceptual modes, and a wide range of inquiry across disciplines that are no longer based exclusively on the object, perhaps in hindsight we ought to include the apparatus that helped fabricate the art as an equal agent, a co-object, enabling object, sidekick. When he first began to publish his research on the theory, Hockney used Roy Lichtenstein's painting *Image Duplicator*

(1963), (itself a copy of Jack Kirby's comic style with its frowning, super-villain face [Magneto] and text bubble), to ask *What? Why did you ask that? What do you know about my image duplicator?*

As much as I'm implying that this exhibition is related to a long history of tech-assisted approaches to the production of art objects, the results here are significantly different – they are not exactly instruments to help perceive something (or are they?): they are more like a series of test-cases for object-integrated *extensions*, or functional enhancements that seem to meet a need for multiple vantage points. They "pop up" to demonstrate something, like a ginsu knife might demonstrate unparalleled sharpness. It's as if there's a problem-solving rationale behind each one – now that we can model the object in this way, how does it help us troubleshoot potential design flaws? (If there are aspects of advertising or product-pitching that seem not too distant, we should not be surprised. There is also much in common with the related development of games and toys, especially drones.) Furthermore, the whole point of the Call for Art was to ask artists to specifically use an emerging digital technology (augmented reality – as differentiated from virtual reality, a Holodeck-like immersive experience) that both artist an audience accept openly, without any attempt to conceal or minimize the role played by this enabling tool, this agency that transforms the work into a simulacrum (a copy of a copy with no firm sense of an 'original' in the traditional sense).

The range of artists, from painters to sculptors to designers and architects, in a relatively small total submission sample, is also worth noting. Most did not create new work for the exhibition but adapted existing works to the transformation. The central role of R ay Freeman – including the biographical experience he outlines in his essay – is mirrored in his deep involvement with many of these projects, in some cases creating them himself with "direction" from or discussion with the artist. In some cases, the artists here did not 'make' anything but transmitted an idea for something to be made. Ray's own contribution – a rendition of a hole, an opening into the page (a pop-down pop-up) – is meant to be instructive, to demonstrate the potential of the application. The Pop-Up book format also exerts an influence or gravity – archival, curatorial and experimental – yet *the author* does not see himself explicitly as a curator and in fact thanks the jurors for serving that role. (P rior to this project, Freeman designed a fist-sized robot equipped with a paintbrush that upon receiving commands for movement patterns, would proceed to busily cover a surface with marks.)

Ethically, there is an elitist aspect in the requirement of owning an interface device ($300 - $400 plus $100 or more monthly service) without which the artwork is not viewable (although the app, at least, is available for free download), but to some extent this same critique can be made for much of the new media genre. (And yet it is absent from the otherwise astute review of new media aesthetics considered by F rancisco Ricardo in *The Engagement Aesthetic: Experiencing New Media Art Through Critique*, 2013). Introducing the implications for the future, Ricardo nicely captures a sense of why such experiments matter:

> And so it is that art now follows media. …
> Consequently, museums and publications devoted to art regard the image in its new feral contexts. The art image in contemporary work may still be framed and hanging on the gallery wall, but it now disregards that context and operates as a window to worlds that are far from where art *was*." (Ricardo's emphasis, ibid., 4)

While this project was initially conceived as a virtual exhibition, thereby assuaging CoCA's ongoing lack of a stable physical space, it has morphed into a physical component after all. F rom the street, gazing into the exhibition through the windows, however, visitors will see only a series of empty pedestals, where the art *will be* when the doors open and devices are scanned over surfaces.

As for the results, the technology is by no means perfect

(there are lighting constraints and stability issues) but given the range of field conditions, it works surprisingly well nevertheless, conjuring a ghostly image above the phone that one holds closely to inspect, turning it to examine angles…For the uninitiated (like myself), let it be stated that the apparition of the object in thin air above one's device is *not a reproduction of an artist's drawing (in 3-D) or sculpture*; it is a unique object that is triggered or manifested (*ins Leben gerufen*, brought into being) by embedded information in the page.

Inevitably, Walter Benjamin's 1936 essay on art and mechanical reproduction will loom ever-larger as these pages are turned. In the twilight of what Benjamin called art's "aura," the means of making facsimiles nudges art's production into politics and broadly defined cultural spheres (social practice; performance; the artist as social worker more than producer of commodity -objects). Returning to the executive summary offered at the outset, it may be the case that after viewing these experiments, we ask, is it art? What new phase of curating is this? Yet these are semantic questions to some extent in the context of larger discoveries regarding our encounter, 100 years after Duchamp's readymades, with the 'made thing,' (from Greek: τέχνη, *techne*), that derives from us yet looks back at its creator with a strange form of autonomy that defies simple categorization as imitation, reproduction, or representation.

Working primarily as an independent curator for the past decade, former CoCA board member David Francis continues to explore a multi-disciplinary practice in poetics, visual art, and archæology. After MFA and PhD degrees in poetry and critical theory , he lectured in Poland and Hungary on several Fulbright grants before teaching at Cornish College of the Arts from 1999 - 2006. Recent curatorial work at Museum of Glass and Museum of Northwest Art has led him to his current post as Public Art Coordinator for the City of Shoreline.

The Call for Art
CoCA Pop-Up (AR)t Book
A Book of Augmented Reality Artwork

This Call for Art appeared on the CoCA website from October 3, 2015 through November 29, 2015, and was shared with media and other arts oranizations around the country.

Over the course of about two months, 35 submissions were received from eight states and four countries.

Center on Contemporary Art invites 3D artists to submit works for consideration in an upcoming A ugmented Reality Popup Book. This is part of ongoing effort to push the boundaries of Contemporary Art - in this case by bringing new technology to our publishing effort, and seeing what you might be inspired to do!

WHAT IS IT?

Like a traditional pop-up book, three dimensional versions of the featured artwork will spring to life as the viewer turns the page, using a special software-driven Augmented Reality feature that allows the viewer to see the work in three dimensions on their own mobile device – iPhone, iPad, Android device, etc. Links to the required software will be included in the book and on the web.

WHAT ARE WE LOOKING FOR?

Works can be existing, physical or virtual, proposed, imaginary, conceptual, experimental, or any combination of these. Works that push the boundaries of the AR concept are encouraged, and do not have to be physically possible or technically constructible. Some animation of the model may be possible.

Each selected work will be represented in images, words, and in an embedded 3D model. Consequently, the work to be considered must be physically or virtually three-dimensional, and able to be modeled in a 3D computer program.

WHAT DO YOU SUBMIT?

Submission materials can take the form of photos, sketches, renderings, or any other way that you can communicate your idea in submitted images and text. If your work is selected, we will work with you to get it modeled for the AR feature of the book. You do not need to be a computer artist to submit. However, if you are capable of creating your own model in .3ds, .max, .dxf , or .fbx or other polygon based 3D format (even Sketch-Up), please note that in your submission. It will make our job that much easier!

WHO DECIDES WHAT GOES IN?

12 to 20 works will be selected by CoCA Publisher Ray C. Freeman III, CoCA Curatorial Advisor David Francis, and CoCA Board Member and Past President Joseph C. Roberts.

WHAT'S THE SCHEDULE?

Call for Entries Deadline for submissions was Sunday, November 29, midnight PST.

Selections will be made by December 30. We may need to work with submitting artists in the interim to ensure that their works are feasible for the book concept and technology. Due to this additional step, production of the book, including 3D model development, is anticipate to take 90 days or more.

The Software
Use the Wikitude App to View the Pop-Up Artwork

This book presents virtual pop-up artwork by eighteen artists exploring varying aspects of what that means.

To take advantage of the experience presented in this volume requires the use of an application running on your smart phone or tablet running iOS or Android.

The app, *Wikitude*, is available at the Apple App Store or through Google Play, and is a free download. In the App, search for *CoCA Pop Up (AR)t Book* to view the 3D artwork by pointing your device's camera at the square image in the upper right corner of each right-hand page.

Simply follow the instructions on the right to download the software, search for this book, and view the 3D images.

Here are some tips for achieving the best results:

1. Keep the page flat. The software might not be able to recognize the target image if it is curved or bent.

2. Make sure you have adequate, even light and there are no shadows cast on the target image.

3. When you are first viewing an arwork, point directly at the target image, or at a slight angle, rather than at a steep angle.

4. Some of the files are larger than others, and will take longer to load. Be patient! Once the model has loaded, if will load much more quickly the next time if you accidentally lose the target out of frame.

5. Move your device around the image or spin the book to see the artwork from all sides. Remember to keep the target image in the frame, or the software might lose track of the model. You can even back away from the target and see more of the model, and you can tilt the book somewhat to see the model at "eye level".

Viewing the artwork in three easy steps:

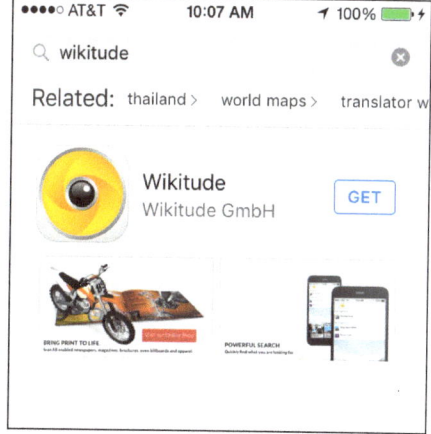

1. Download the Wikitude app from the Apple App Store or Google Play

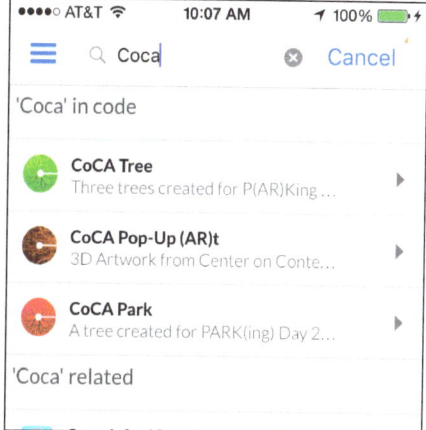

2. In the App, type "Coca" into the search bar and select "CoCA Pop-Up (AR)t" from the search results

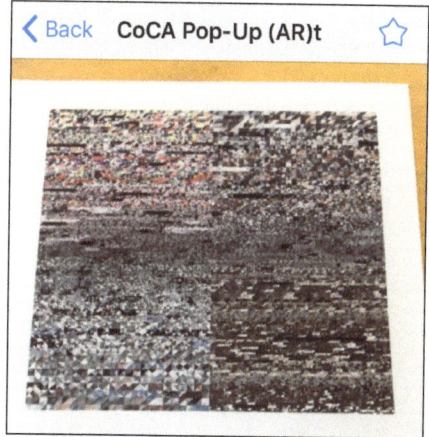

3. View the target image through the app, wait for the artwork to appear!

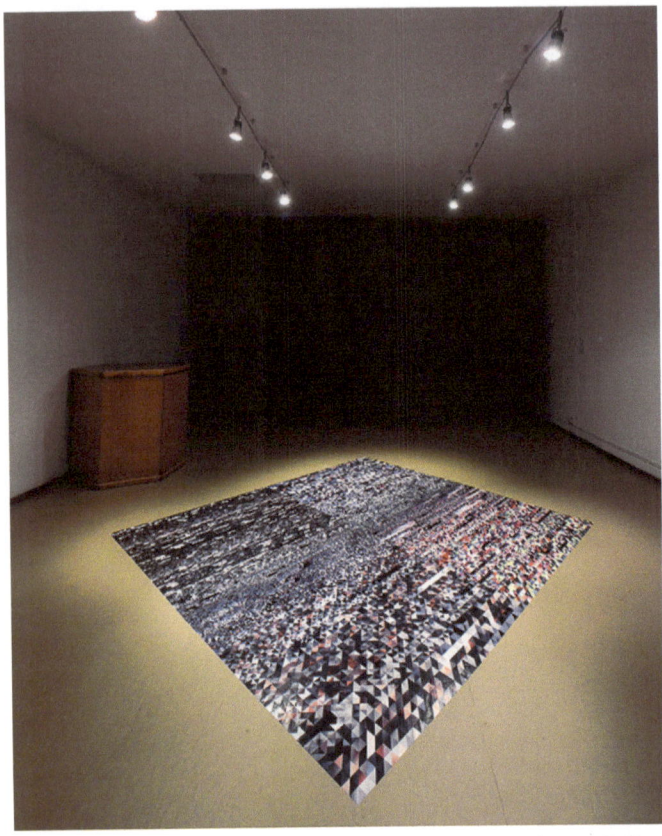

This is a panaroma of this work installed at the Dendroica Gallery on Capitol Hill. The image is 6' x 6', consisting of 4 x 3' x 3' adhesive vinyl prints to make one large image target for AR tracking.

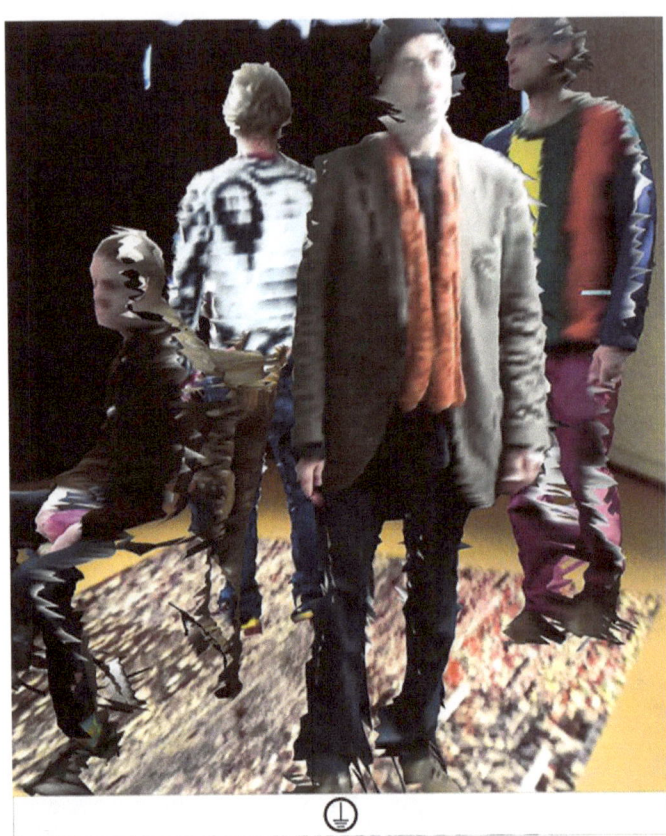

This is a screen grab from a ipad Mini running the software I developed. Humans are rendered and played back to scale within the space of the installation.

The work consists of an AR mobile application and four or more generative prints that are combined together to make one large image in the center of a given space. The mobile application will be available for free through the Apple and Android stores, being fully supported on all modern iPhone and Android devices, including the Oculus Gear VR. The images are printed on a vinyl adhesive sticker that is adhered to a floor for viewers to safely walk upon. The prints are renderings of people who have been 3D scanned followed by texture unwrapped into an abstract array of colored triangles.

I'm calling these images Brane-Xels. Branes are objects described in physics with varying dynamic properties and dimensions, a brane can even be a dimension or an entire cosmos. Xels comes from pixel which is a combination of picture and element, in this case being an element, or xel, of a brane. The brane-xels effectively are the two dimensional bits of the higher dimensional holographic people they emit. When a user points their mobile device at one of the prints, a to scale augmented voxel video portrait of a person appears that can be viewed from any angle when still having the target image in view. Multiple images can be viewed simultaneously and multiple users can share the same augmented content from their own unique perspectives.

Reilly Donovan – Digital Media Artist, extensive experience in creative conception, development, management, & delivery of international contemporary art installations involving new media technologies.

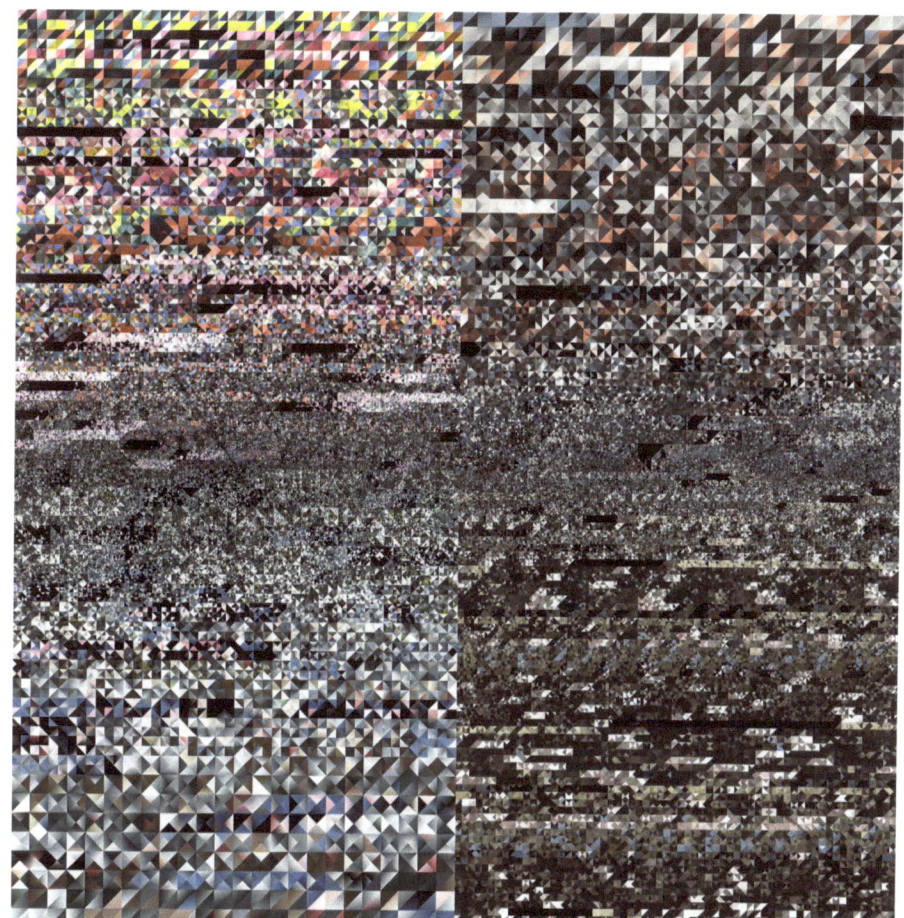

Brane-Xels
Reilly Donovan

Brane-Xels is an exploration into the relationship between developing cosmic theories and emerging forms of visual art portraiture experienced through the canvas of augmented reality. The work integrates generative prints, depth video, and mobile devices to create life-size holographic portraits of people. The portraits are inspired by the information loss paradox and the holographic principle, which are emerging explanations within theoretical physics for what happens to information when it enters a black hole.

reillydonovan.com

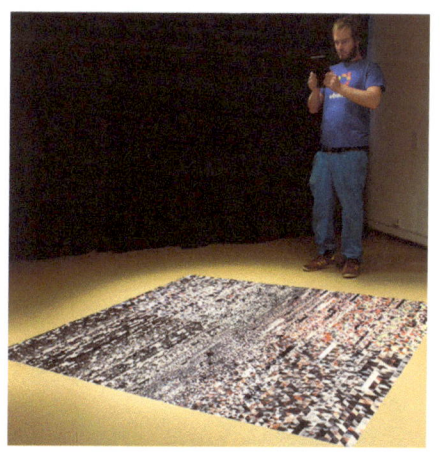
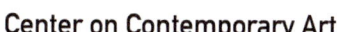

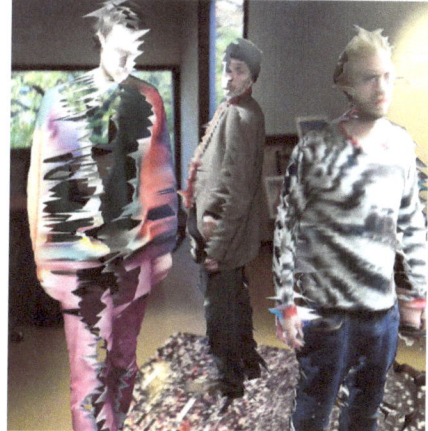

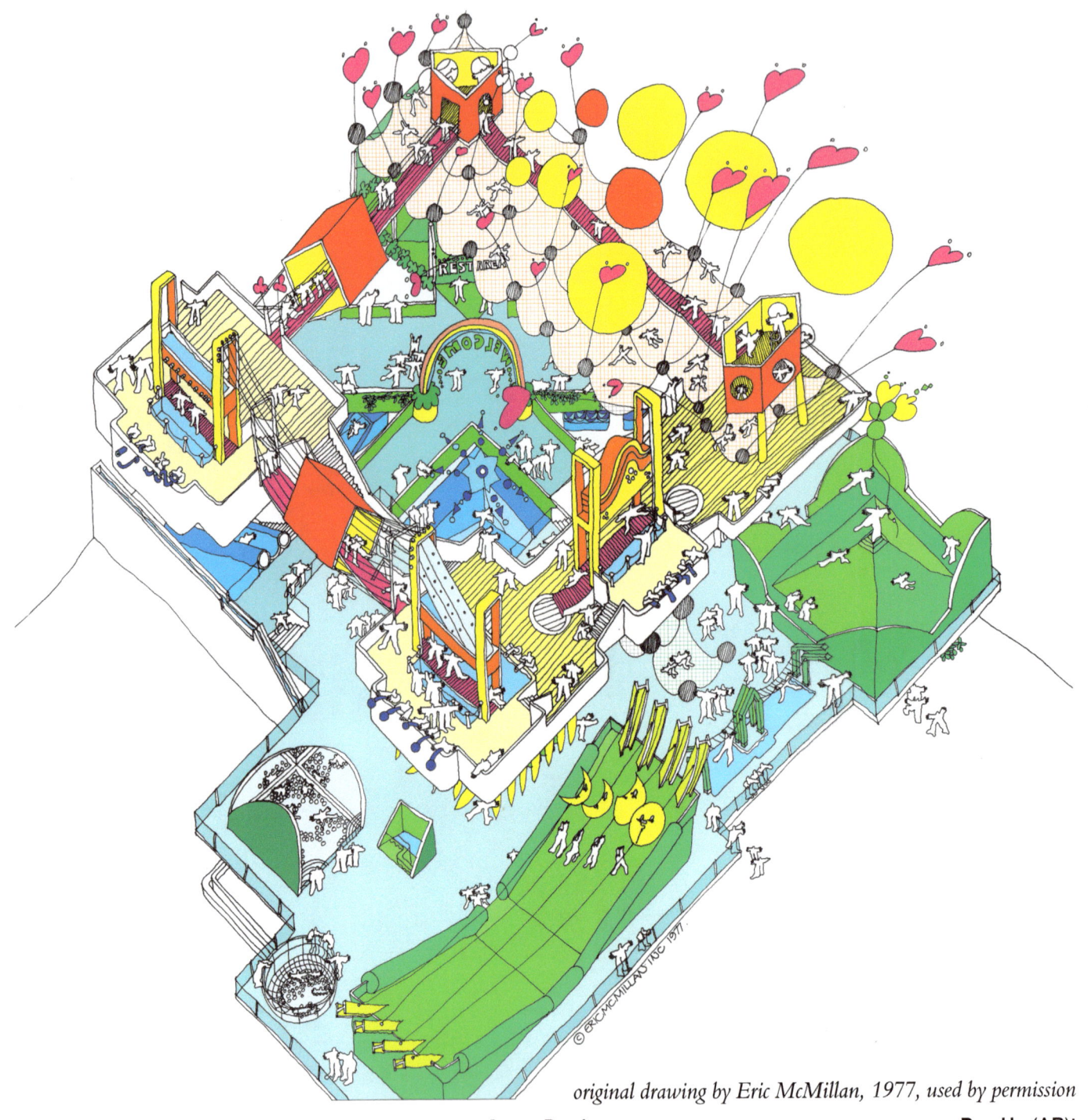

original drawing by Eric McMillan, 1977, used by permission

Corey Dunlap

Pop Up (AR)t

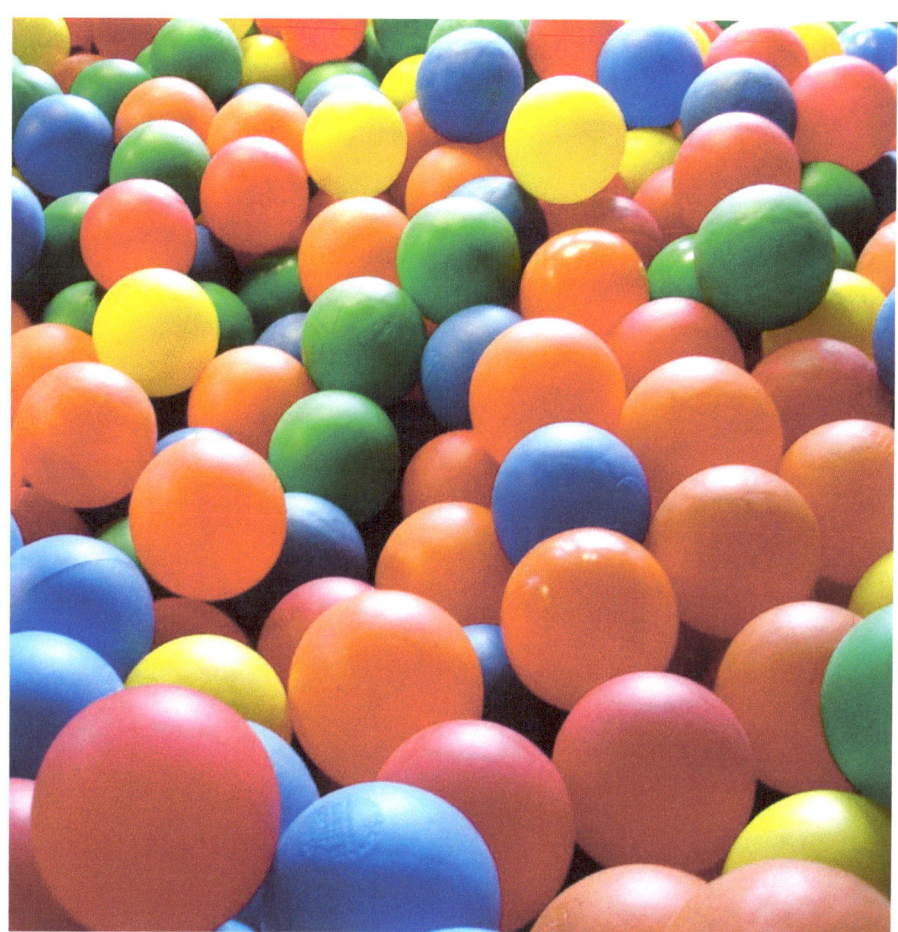

Torus 2
Corey Dunlap

My submission consists of a digital illustration based on the designs of Eric McMillan. With as much structural accuracy as possible, I have reproduced Mr. Mcmillan's drawing as a three-dimensional model in the program Blender. I have removed all color from the illustration, leaving only a homogeneous black, white, and grey scale to differentiate form. In addition, figures based in the original illustration are replaced with a torus or "doughnut" form to represent the body. This torus form is both referential of the set of base structures available in many 3D modeling programs, as well as being a provocative method for understanding the structure of the human body; we essentially have a hole running through us and therefore, can be conceived as a complex torus.

Eric McMillan is a Canadian play designer who worked primarily in the 1970's and 80's in America and Europe. Throughout his career Mr. Mcmillan pioneered the construction of many interactive play environments in theme parks, water parks, and public playgrounds. Many contemporary play centers, from Chuck E. Cheese to Six Flags, utilize perversions of his designs.

Today's play design and interactive landscapes are born from the virtual world, constructed through advanced 3D modeling programs, engaging the body through a series of reductive geometric forms. At the time when Eric McMillan was working no such technology existed, and he in turn constructed a series of illustrative drawings to document his projects.

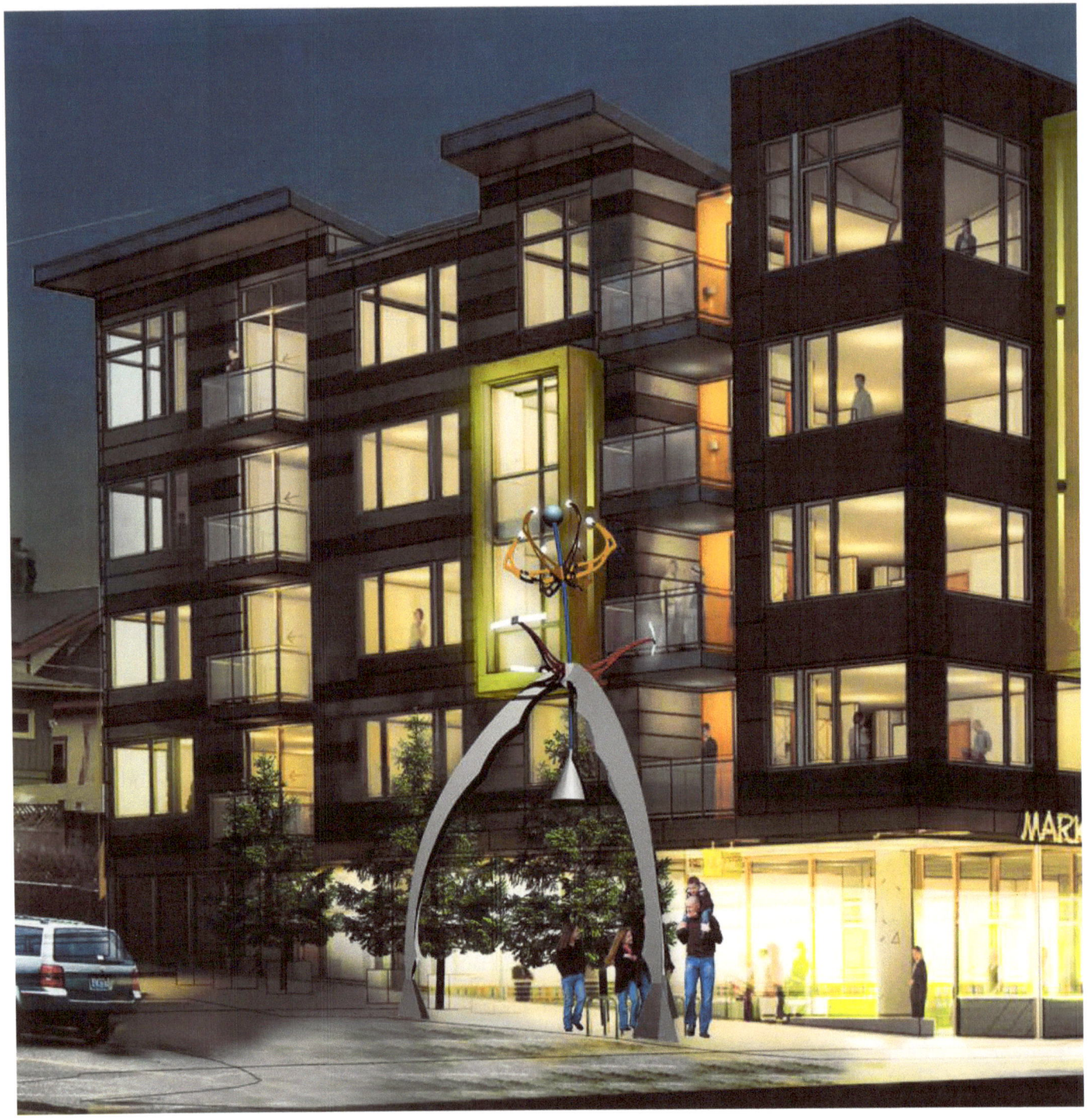

Miguel Edwards

Pop Up (AR)t

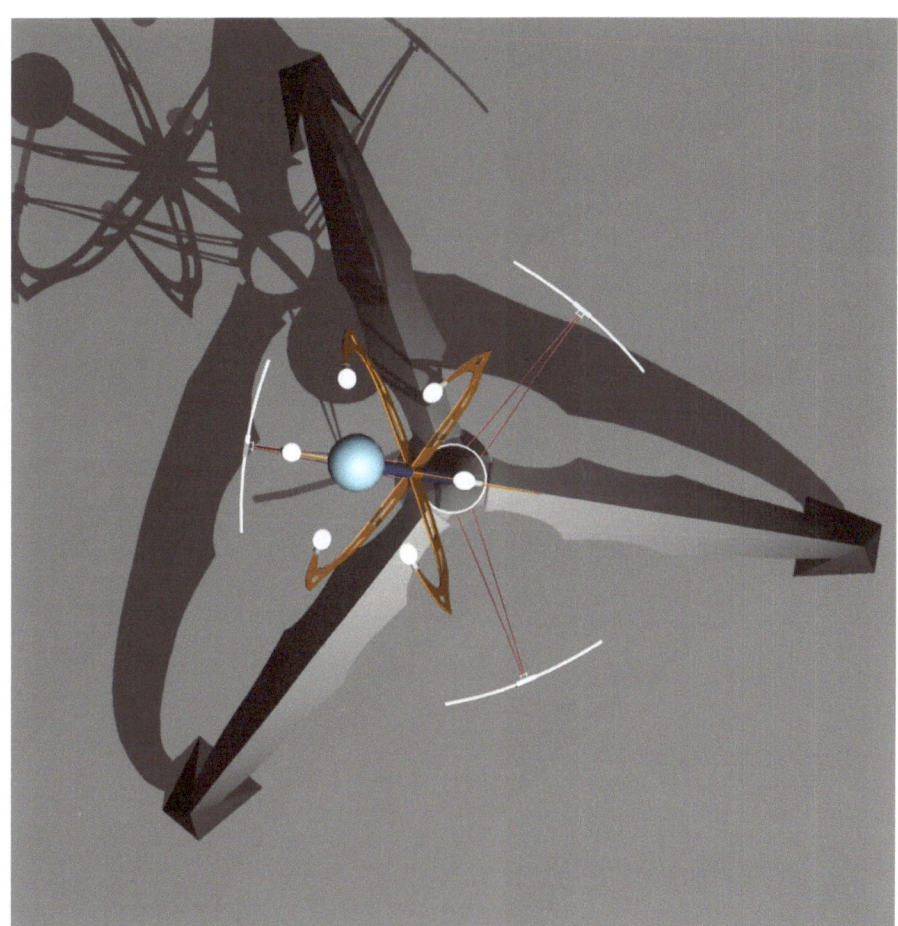

Perseus II
Miguel Edwards

This image is a rendering of Perseus II, the next evolution of my large-scale kinetic interactive sculptures. In the course of creating a public art proposal for Security Properties in Seattle, Ray C. Freeman III built this beautiful 3D model, which was part of his inspiration for this book.

The proposal was accepted and I am currently halfway through building this 3 story tall stainless steel, glass, and LED kinetic interactive sculpture that will straddle the sidewalk at the intersection of NW 85th St & 1st Ave NW, and pierce the awning of the building known as Janus.

Perseus I, one of my more successful public works, was in CoCA's Heaven and Earth II Exhibition at Carkeek Park in 2010. I am very excited about the continuation of the legacy. I hope that Perseus II will be loved for many decades by people of all walks of life, and begin some meaningful conversations as our city grows and evolves.

I embrace concurrent evolutions of visual wanderlust. Time, chaos and intuition are the co-conspirators in my creative process. I constantly investigate new ways to explore beauty, and to bring forward hidden common denominators in the world we perceive.

It is the act of creation that drives and defines my work, as much as it is the finished piece. I try to create artworks that invite everyone to re-discover and indulge? the curiosity and wonder we all had as children: to encourage us to once again see life as full of possibilities and to value our experience in the present.

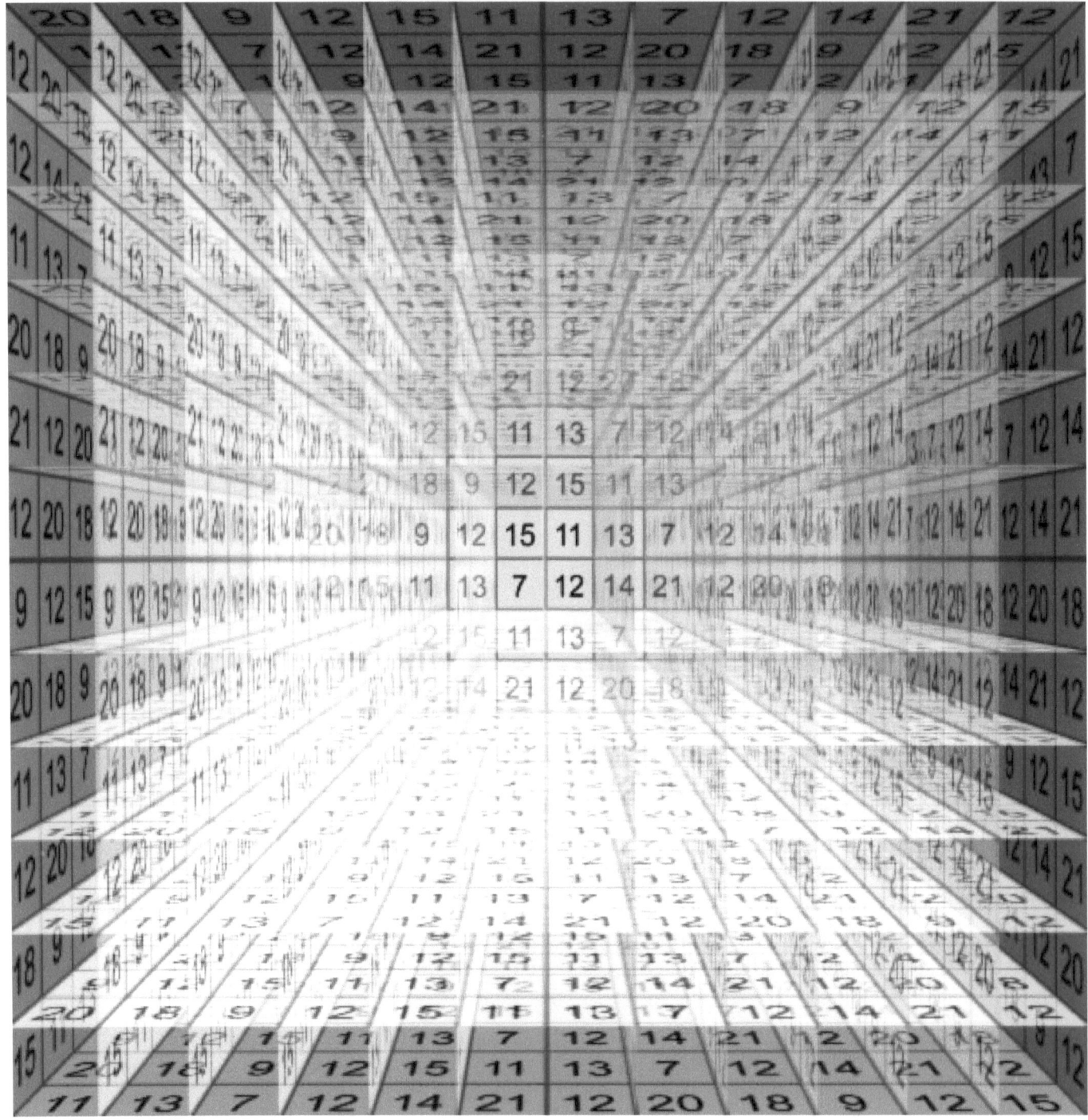

Ray C. Freeman III

Pop Up (AR)t

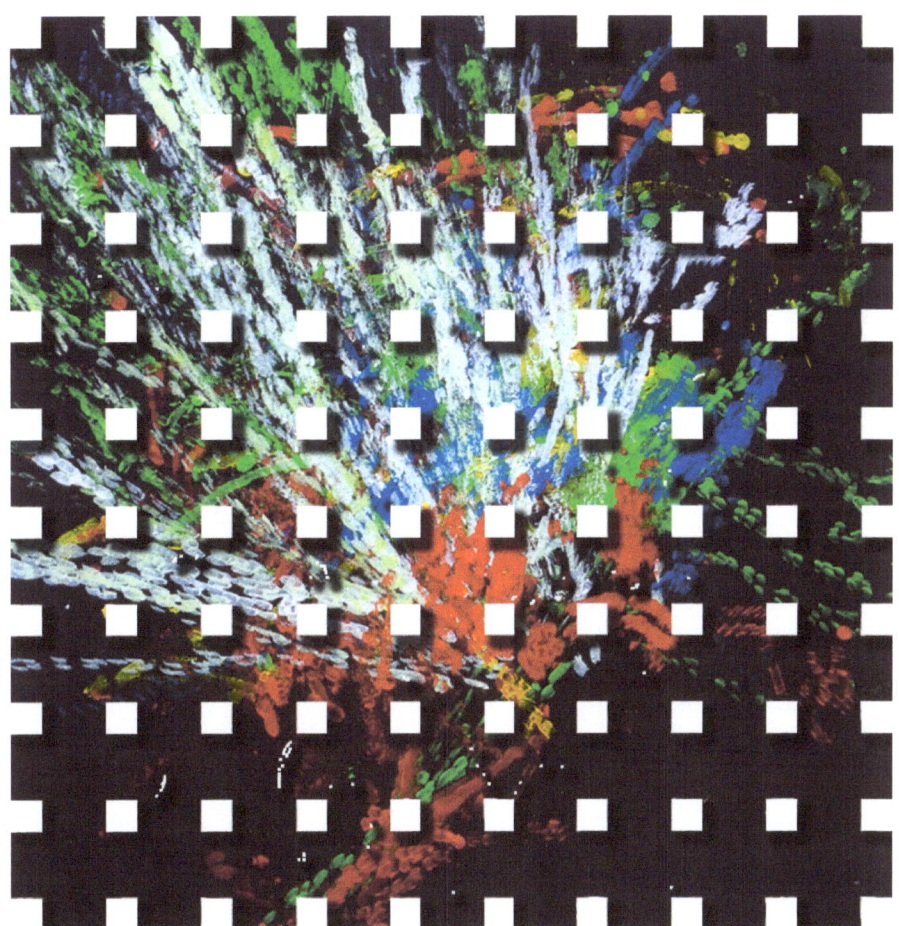

Cube Pit
Ray C. Freeman III

Simple cubes have fascinated me over the years. Some of the most intriguing are cubes made of cubes, spaces filled and therefore defined and organized by cubes, and especially spaces loosely packed with cubes, leaving space between them. These remind me of the nature of matter - that solid materials contain more space that *stuff*.

As the designer of this book, I was also able to explore the relationship of the model to the printed page, including going below the surface of the paper.

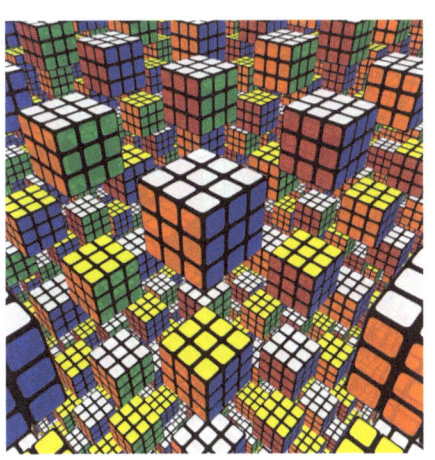

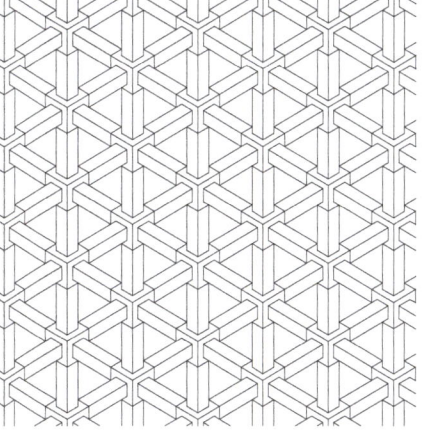

raycfreemaniii.com

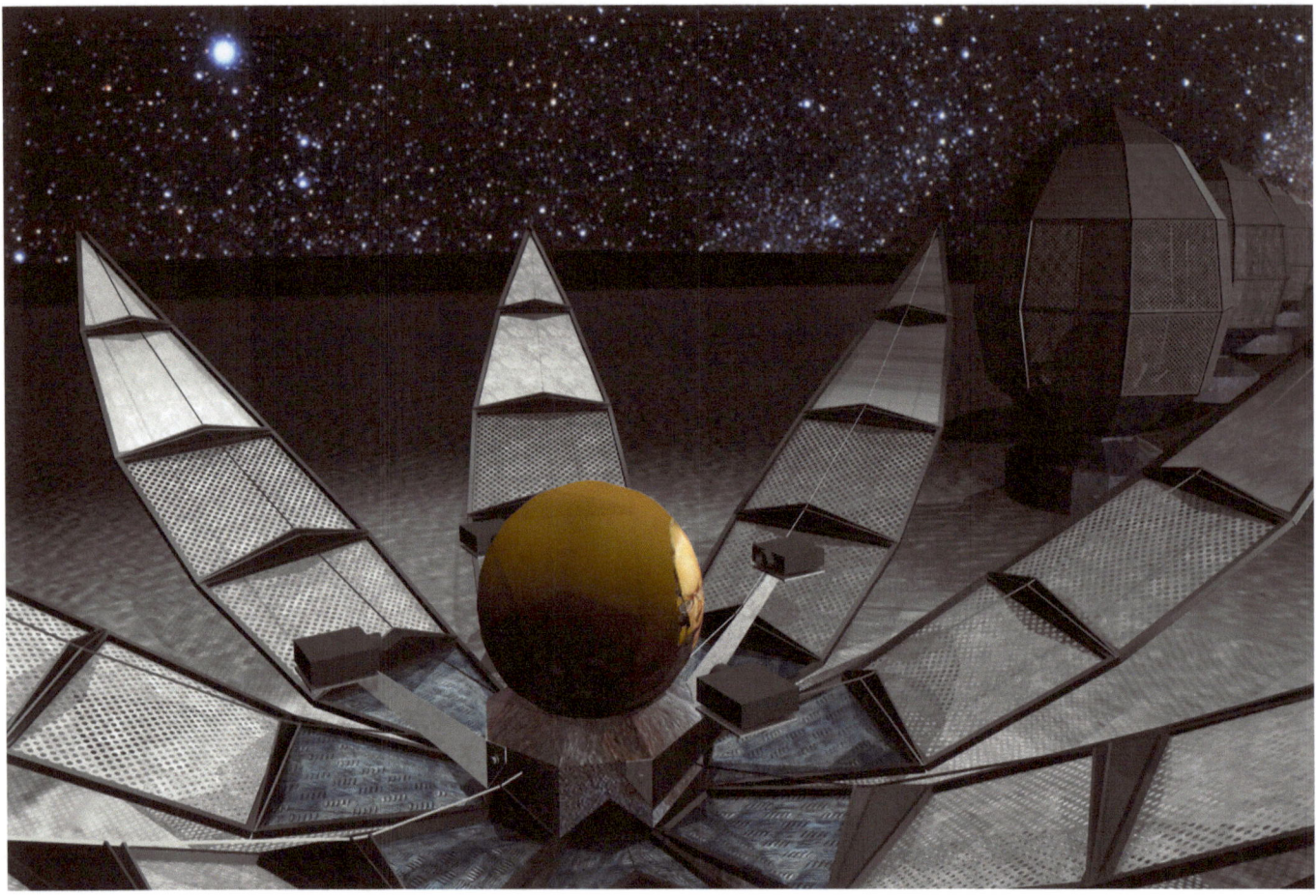

I propose a cosmic communications tool for astronauts to communicate back to Earth and with other astronauts while they're on the moon. Chinese, Russian, and other astronauts, as well as aliens making a pit-stop at the moon before invading Earth, are also invited to use the Cosmic Videophone Booth to phone home and each other.

The artist and assisting astronaut will assemble the Cosmic Videophone Booth, attaching the metal "petals," hooking up the video projectors, filling the base with moon rocks and soil to stabilize it, and activating the solar battery and communication systems.

The pod-like structure, after assembly, stands eight feet tall and resembles a closed flower, its aluminum leaves folded up to protect the video communications sphere inside from asteroids and other dangers. Thin film solar panels, made from amorphous silicon deposited on a polymer substrate, charge the batteries that operate the system.

When communication is desired, as-tronauts use coins or their debit/credit card to place a video call. Payment activates a pulley system of monofilament cables powered by the solar battery that opens the articulated metal petals, blossoming to 16 feet wide and revealing the inflatable, semi-transparent mylar video communications sphere inside.

When the Cosmic Videophone Booth isn't in use, the petals may be folded back up to protect it, or, if desired, comforting scenes of home may be displayed on the video sphere.

Cosmic Videophone Booth
Alan Fulle

Competition Entry

Giant Steps
artist residency on the moon

Bio:

I have been creating sculptures with resin, paint, wood, video, recycled materials, and metal for over two decades. My multi-media practice ranges from traditional to futuristic, abstract to architectural, utilitarian to utopian.

alanfulle.com

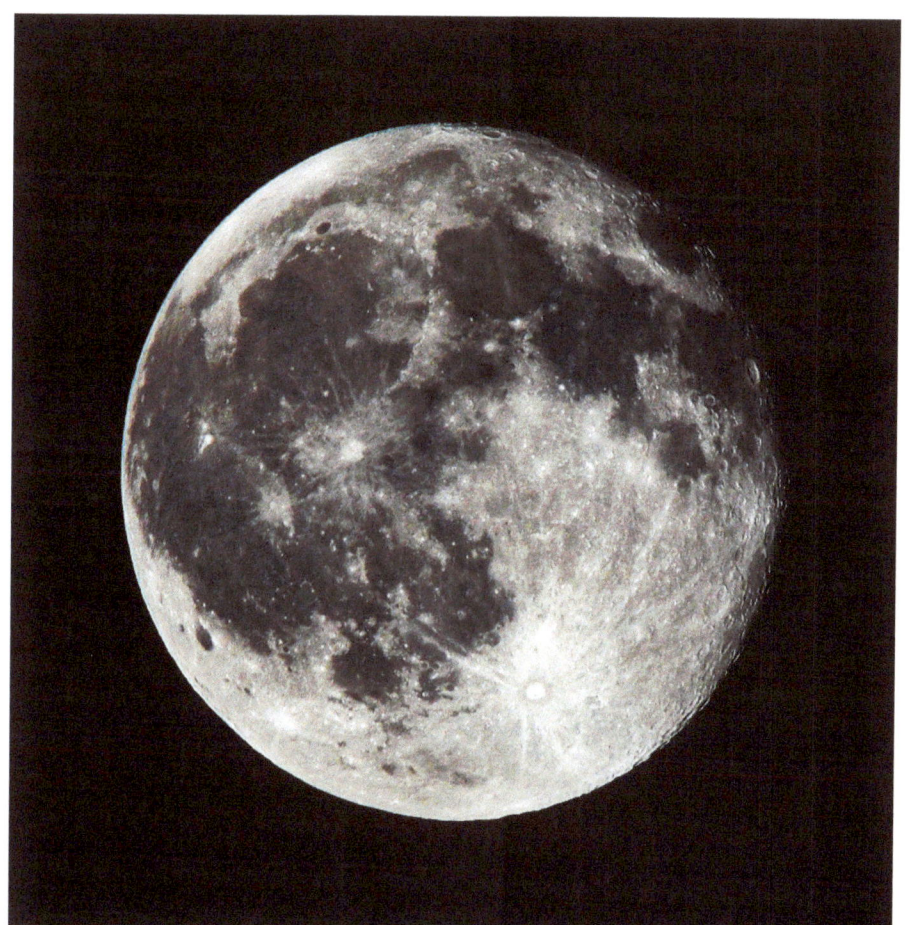

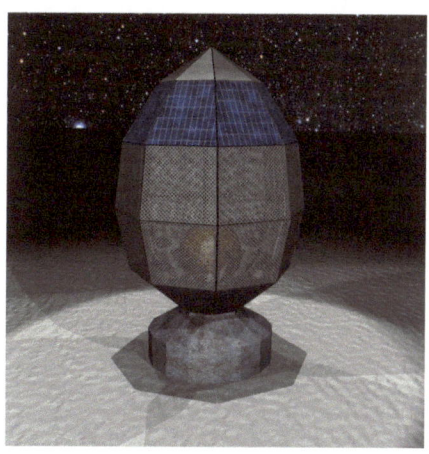

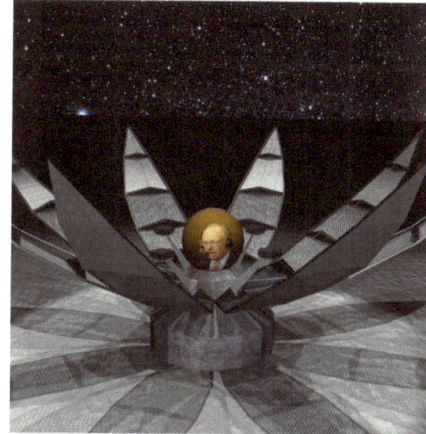

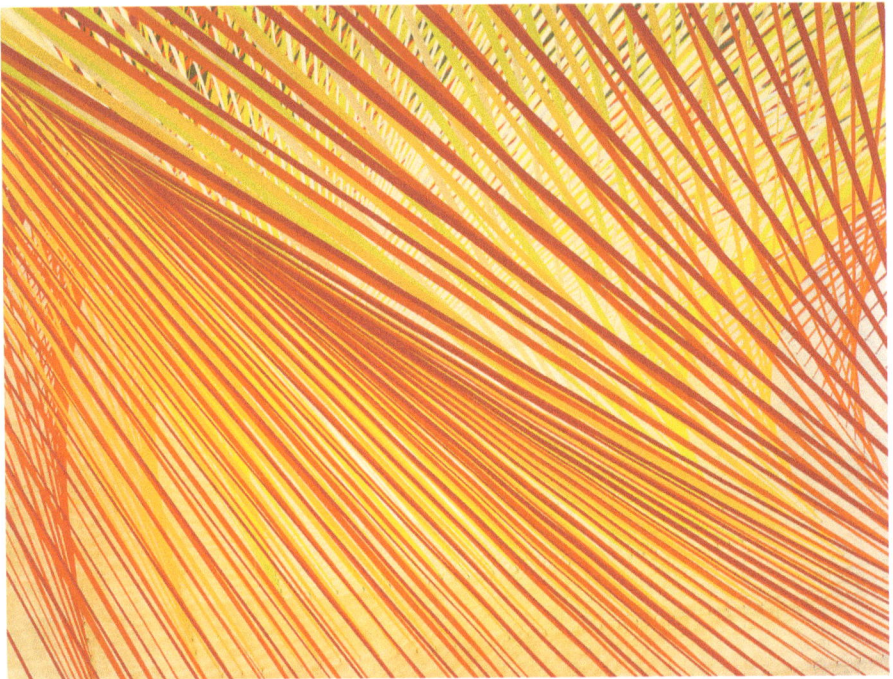

Rewritten by Machine on New Technology ©Megan Geckler

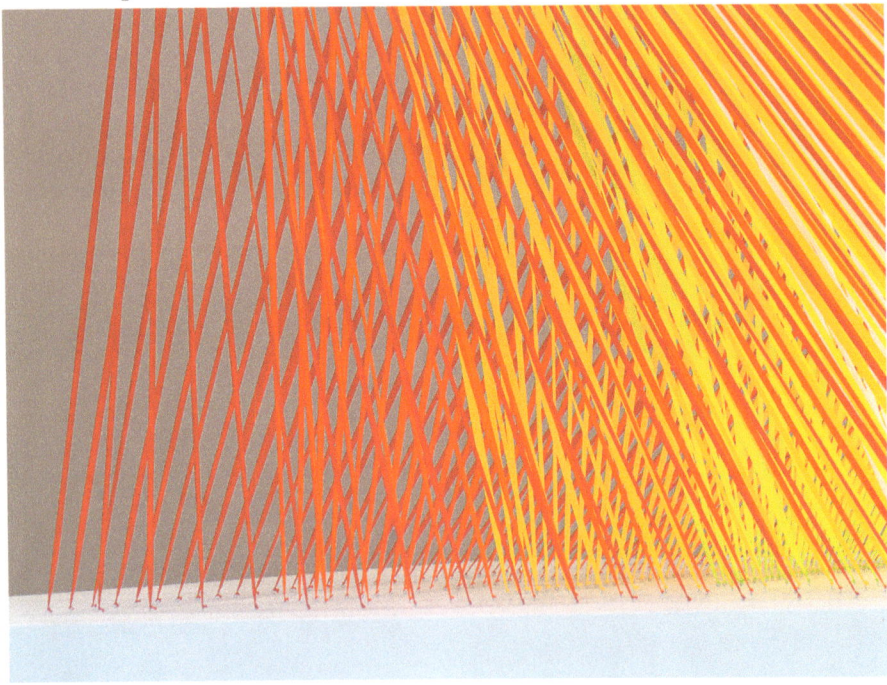

The bulk of my work straddles the fields of fine art, design and craft. Each space in which I work informs the optical order and systematic reasoning that is the foundation for my process. An entryway offers multiple pathways and destinations – each with their own readymade focal point, a soffit becomes the departure point of the piece and the work speaks of the architectural facets and quirks of the space. Upon completion, these architecturally informed site-specific installations share the cool slick look of advertisements, backdrops for fashionable clothing, and high design products. Made of translucent plastic, they simulate and reference our idea of "the future" and camouflage the handmade quality of the work.

Essentially drawings in space, they bisect and alter our perception of the architecture and become seemingly kinetic as the viewer's orientation changes. This phenomenon occurs as a result of the combination of our sensory system with the physics of light. Often disorientation is experienced when the stripe patterns intersect and appear to slide in opposite directions. This fascinates and delights viewers, as they frequently encourage each other to view the work from a certain direction to experience this phenomenon. The end result resembles an updated three-dimensional version of string art that shares the seemingly kinetic territory of the Op Art and Light+Space movements. In this regard, my work is strongly influenced by the paintings of Bridget Riley and the constructions of Naum Gabo. These site-specific projects are also strongly influenced by minimalism, but retain a sense of play and delight.

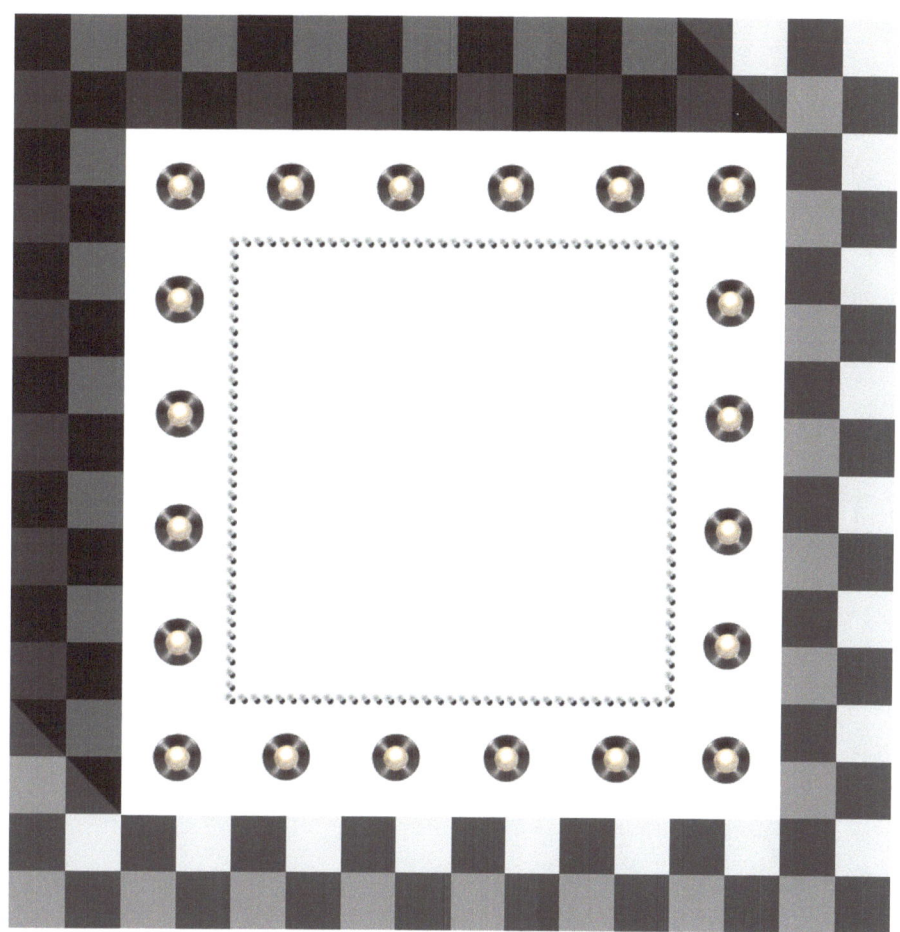

Endless Column
Megan Geckler

This project is based on Constantin Brancusi's "Endless Column" from 1918, a symmetrical element repeated to produce a continuous rhythmic line that emphasized the potential for limitless vertical expansion. Brancusi was never able to realize a true endless column, but via the technology of computer aided design programs – we can. By utilizing an open framework design, instead of the solid wooden form that Brancusi chose, the overlapping lines create dynamic moiré patterns that are unique to each individual's self-guided discovery of the artwork.

Rewritten by Machine on New Technology
©Megan Geckler

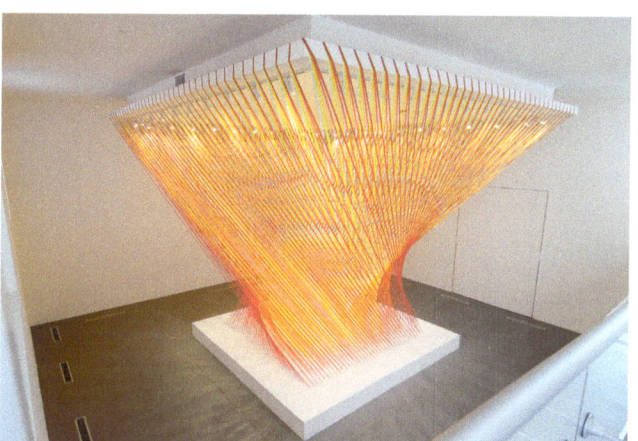

megangeckler.com

Center on Contemporary Art

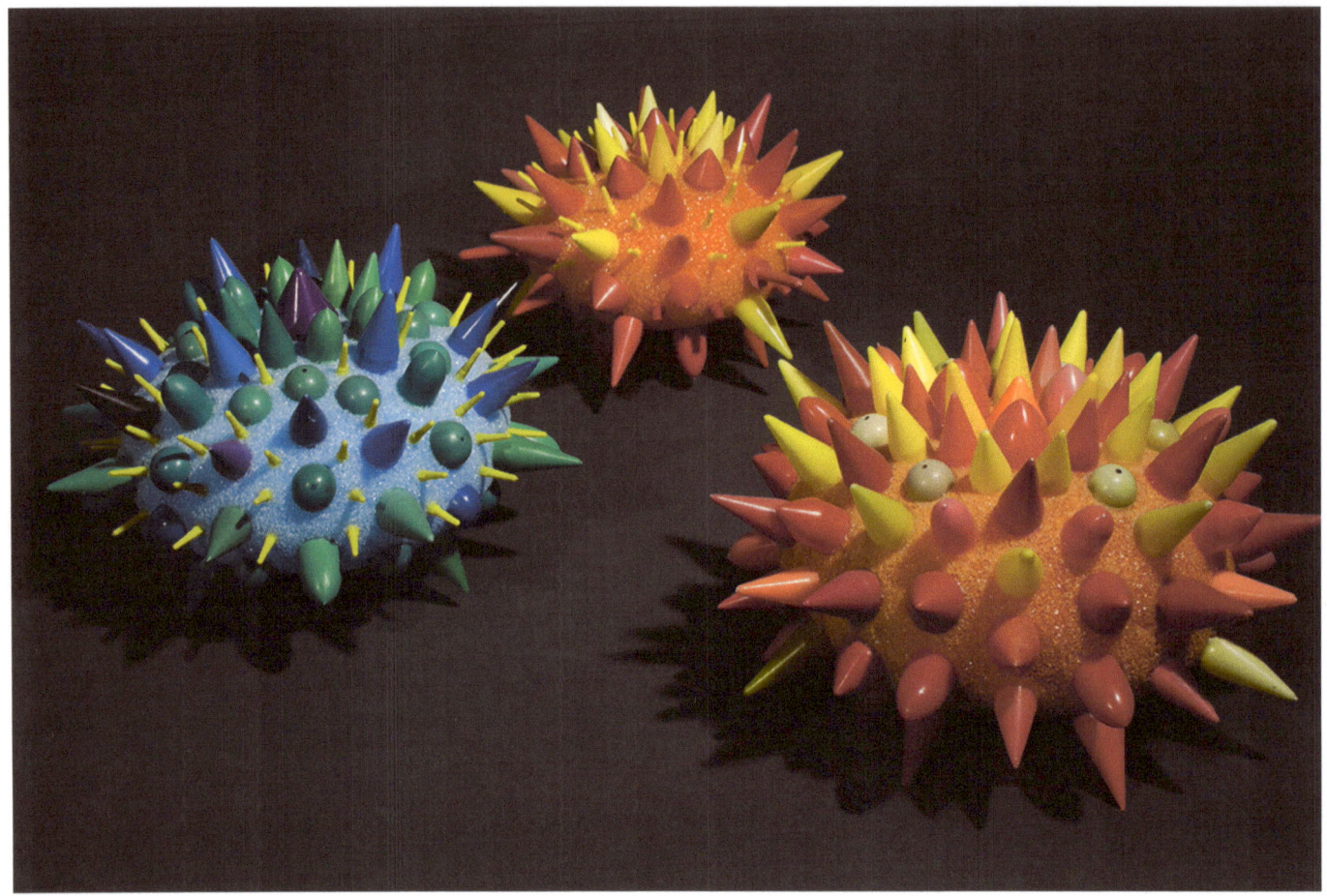

Statement:

Local beach-found flotsam, PETE water bottles, plastic toy animals and product packages are but a few of the found items that I use as subject and medium in my current work.

Painting traditionally with oil and gouache, I lovingly and meticulously craft images of trashed commercial beach flotsam, creating a provocative visual juxtaposition of form and idea.

Using these same cast-off and readymade materials and obsessively repeating them as units of construction, I build plastic bottle and matchstick sculptures that emphasize the relentless insistency of manufacture in relation to healthy environmental economy.

The *American Sea Urchin* series completes the "recycling" theme by re-constituting toxic plastics into mutant sea urchins made from plastic beach debris.

Bio:

Raised in rural Connecticut, Karen Hackenberg developed her first connections to the natural world on the shores of Long Island Sound. She earned her BFA in painting from the Rhode Island School of Design and upon graduating moved west.

After a decade and a half in San Francisco, she migrated to the Pacific Northwest and now lives along the shoreline of Discovery Bay near Port Townsend, Washington.

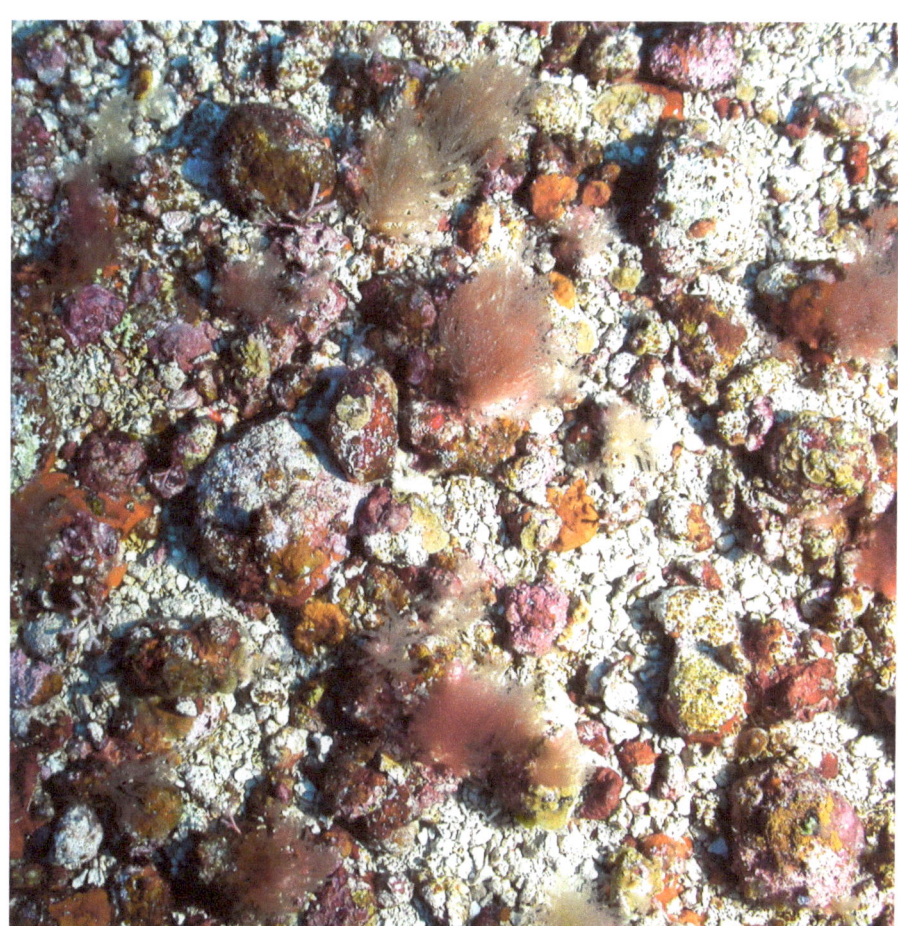

American
Sea Urchin II
Karen Hackenberg

American Sea Urchin II
carved and assembled beach-found
floatation foam and plastic fireworks
tips, 8"x10", 2013.

opposite:

American Sea Urchins I, II, III
a cluster or colony of sea urchins,
2013-2015

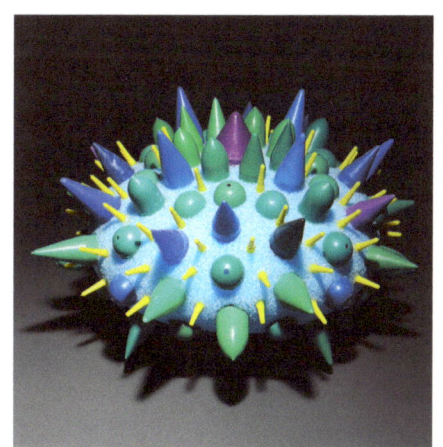

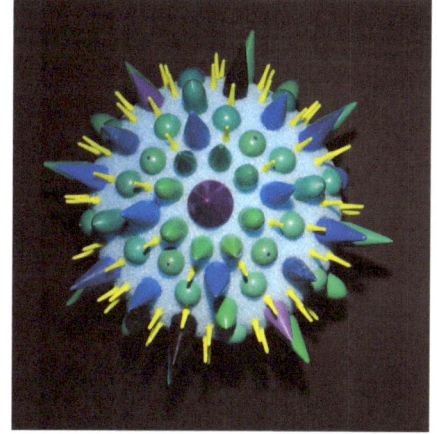

karenhackenberg.com

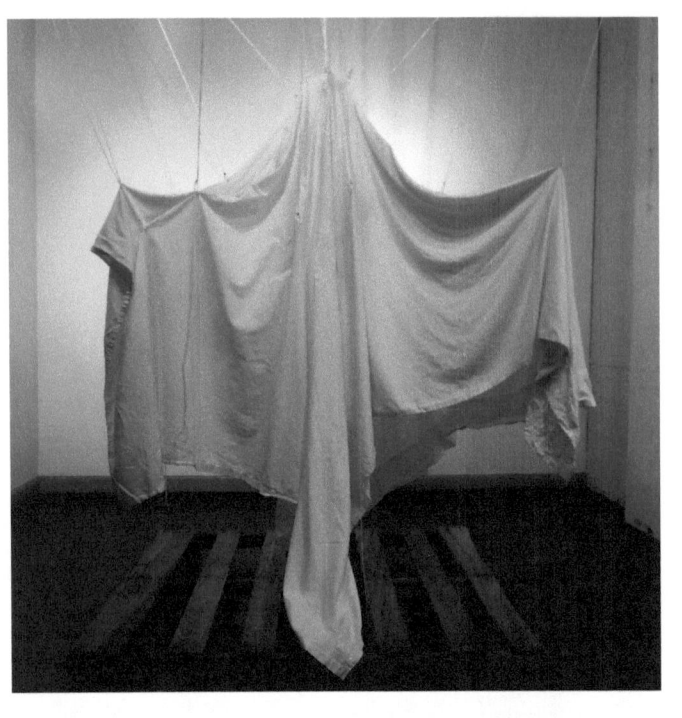 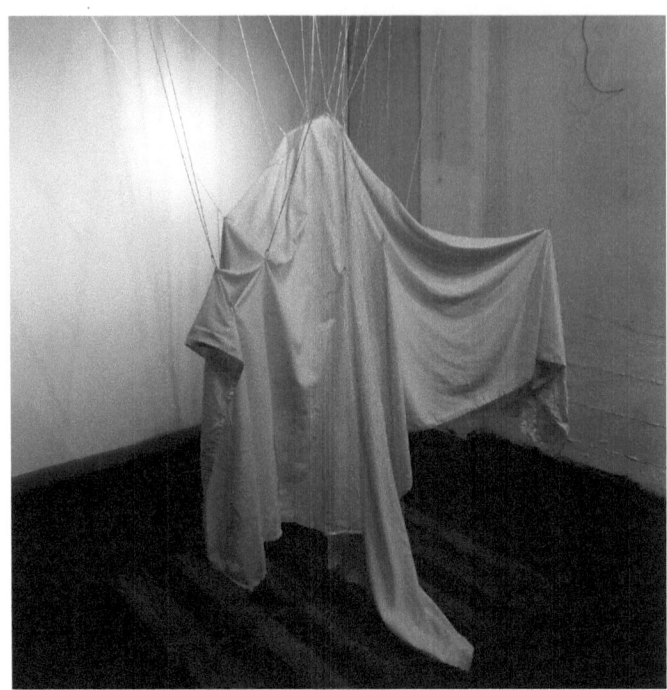

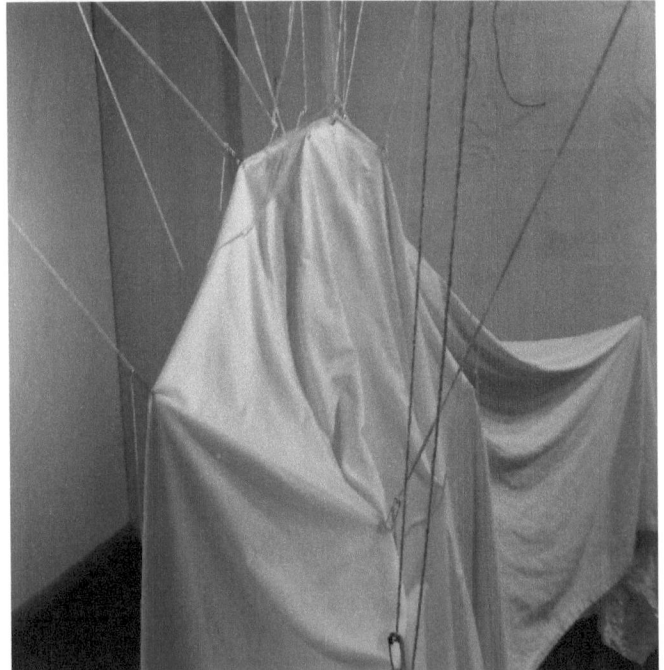 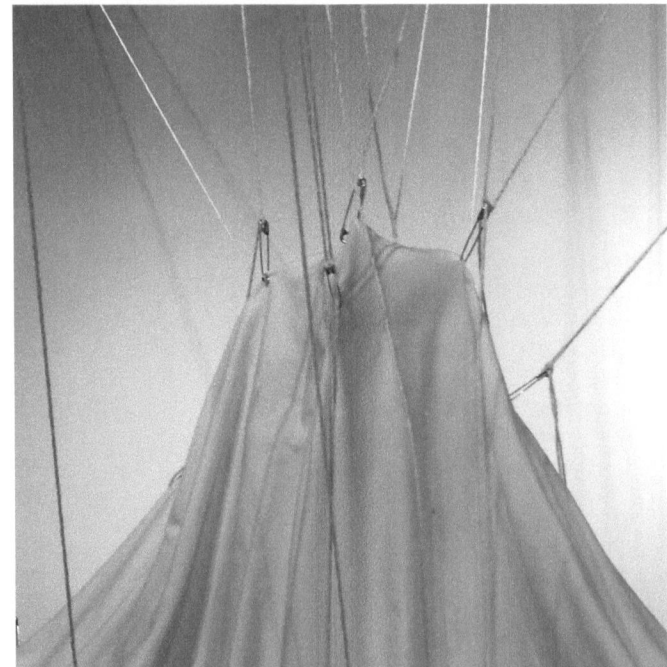

Xavier Lopez Jr. Pop Up (AR)t

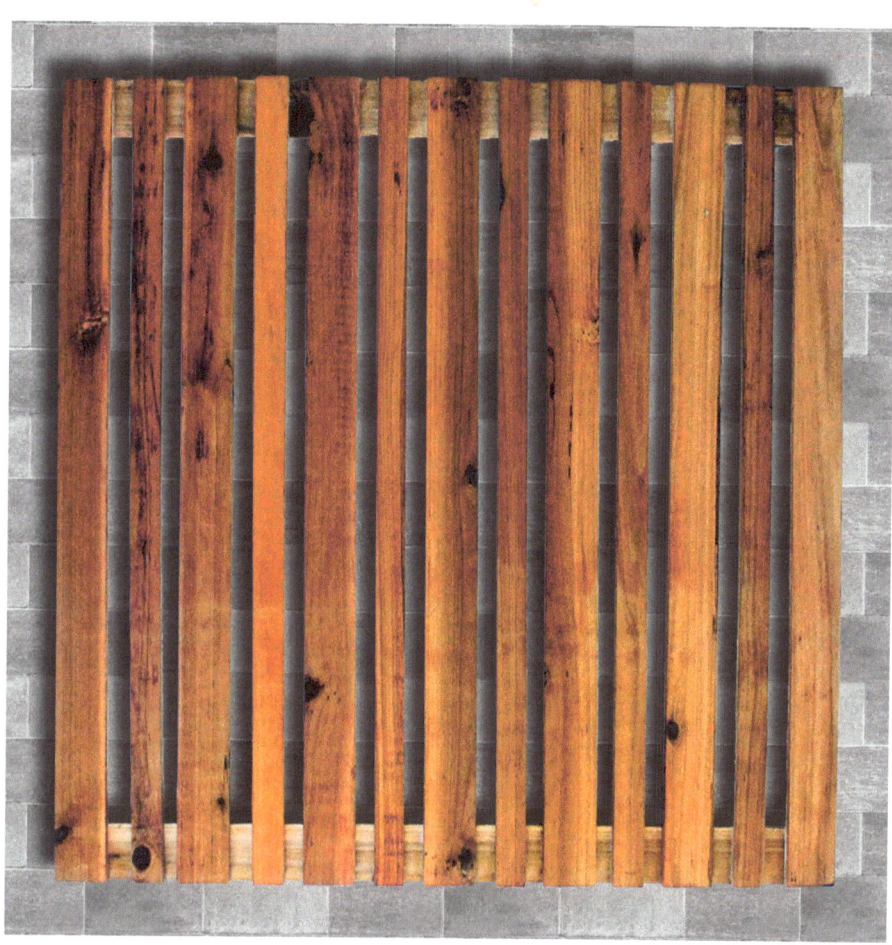

Ghost #3:
Silent Spirit
Xavier Lopez Jr.

There are a few concepts that really guide this sculptural installation, entitled Ghost #3: Silent Spirit. The first being one that has been part of much of my conceptual installation work – and that is the idea of some object or series of objects held together or hanging by strings. The second is that I am attempting to push the idea of "pop." I am seeking to use "pop" imagery in these sculptures, paired down, simplified and purified. In this series, I have been working with the storybook idea of the sheet ghost – which is full of popular ref-erences – from Gus, Georgie and Casper the Friendly Ghost to the Victorian images of ghosts coming from images of old houses with sheets protecting antique objects – which is probably the originary location of the sheet ghost. I have been working with the idea of ghosts in sculpture, per-formance and painting for the last ten years.

In this case, I wanted the sheet ghost to be empty – its shape held together solely by the cords of string stretching up to the ceiling. I wanted the viewer to be able to walk completely around the installation and to be able to peer inside and see that it was absolutely hollow. At the same time, as with most of my sculpture, I wanted it to be minimalist – in essence I see the work as mathematical, with the whole of the object amounting to more than the sum of the parts. The construc-tion is simple, made of a sheet, string, wood, safety pins and eye screws – but the idea that it imparts refers to everything--life, comedy, tragedy, death, childhood, Disneyland, magic, mystery and even sex.

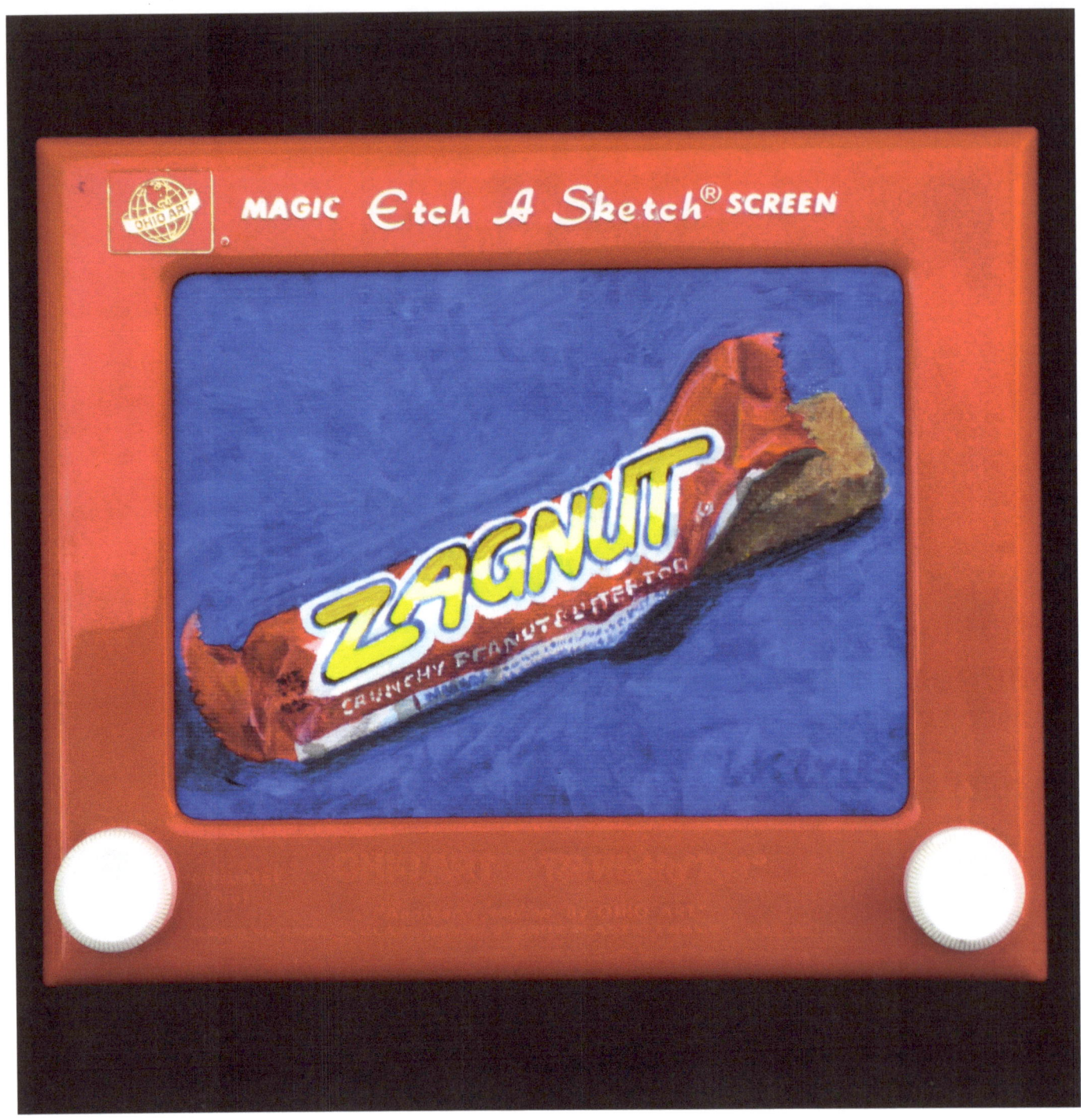

L. Kelly Lyles

Pop Up (AR)t

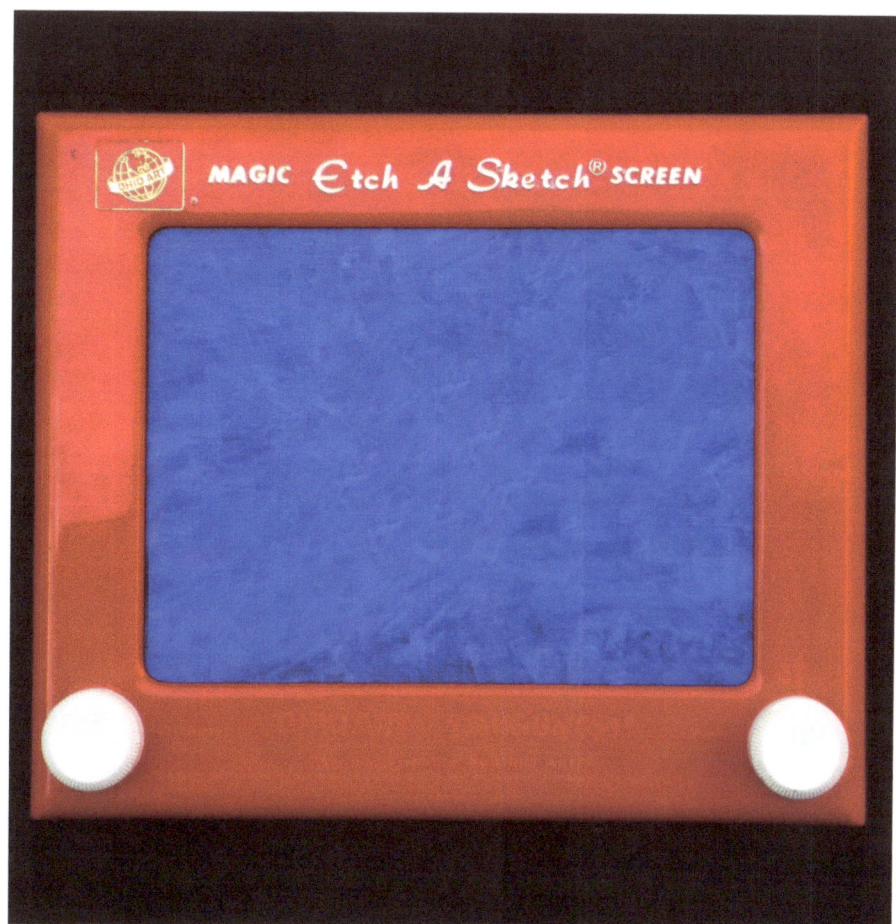

Zag Nut
L. Kelly Lyles

left: Zag Nut (original)
acrylic on canvas board
with Etch-A-Sketch, 9" x 12", 2013

My latest paintings are of Candy: it's colourful, visual, nostalgically evoking childhood memories in a lot of adults (whether it had positive associations, as in rewards or bribes, or conversely the lure of "forbidden fruits" in the stricter households). It's also Universal, all nations share a love of sugary treats, it's a common bond of simple happiness the world over.

But this is a personal theme for me as well as universal - I always keep candy in my studio (as a lure to begin work), and live in fear of the doctor telling me to give up sugar...

I started this series at a fund-raiser for CoCA, the marathon (based on vintage dance marathons) wherein 24 artists work for 24 hours, then our works are sold the next evening at auction. My thinking in choosing candy as subject matter was that I could eat my still-life reference material for the sugar buzz to continue painting the day and night alloted time. It worked beautifully, I was the last one to leave the following morning!

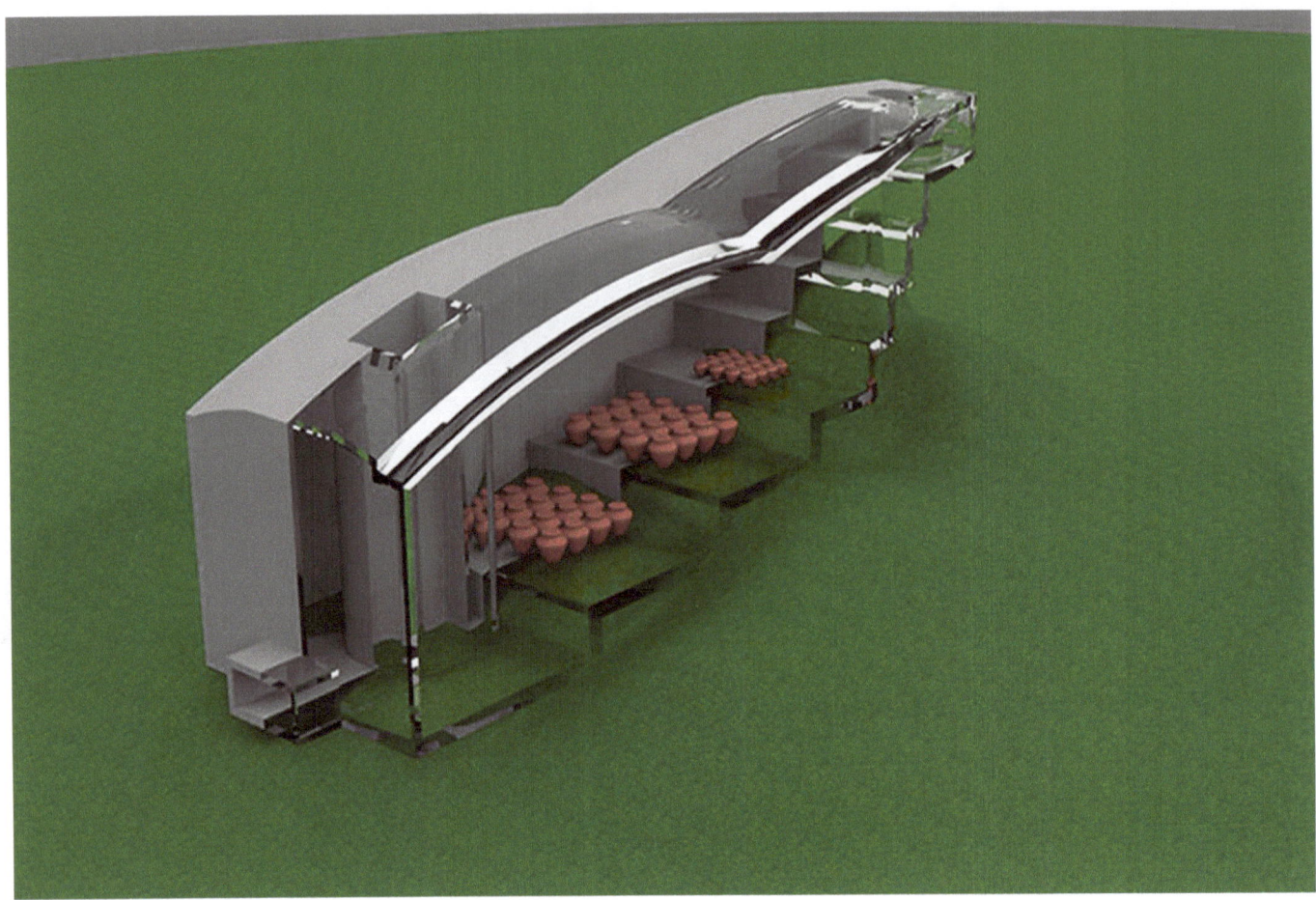

I have pursued my artistic career in the United States with an eye on the increasingly global implications of pluralistic identities. My artistic body of work is informed by interdisciplinarity as well as by cross-cultural exchange between Japan and the West that occurs throughout the history of ceramics.

Historical narratives surrounding particular wares are filled with aesthetic complexities, connections, dialogues, and even cultural clashes.

I am currently interested in systematic representations of scientific approaches to climate change, the concept of satoyama, native and non-native plant species, and environmental management techniques through the use of digital fabrication.

The Mini-kiln project stems from the desire to translate ancient ceramic traditions through the exploration of new technology and strongly relates to AR's vision of an innovative extension of the traditional pop-up book.

The Augmented Reality aspect of this work is that these various components contextualize the history of 'making' in the form of a new kind of "pop-up book," and how AR seeks to challenge how audiences understands object making, history, and technology.

I imagine how the audience could, for example print their own mini-kilns and place them in various landscapes specific to their geographic location.

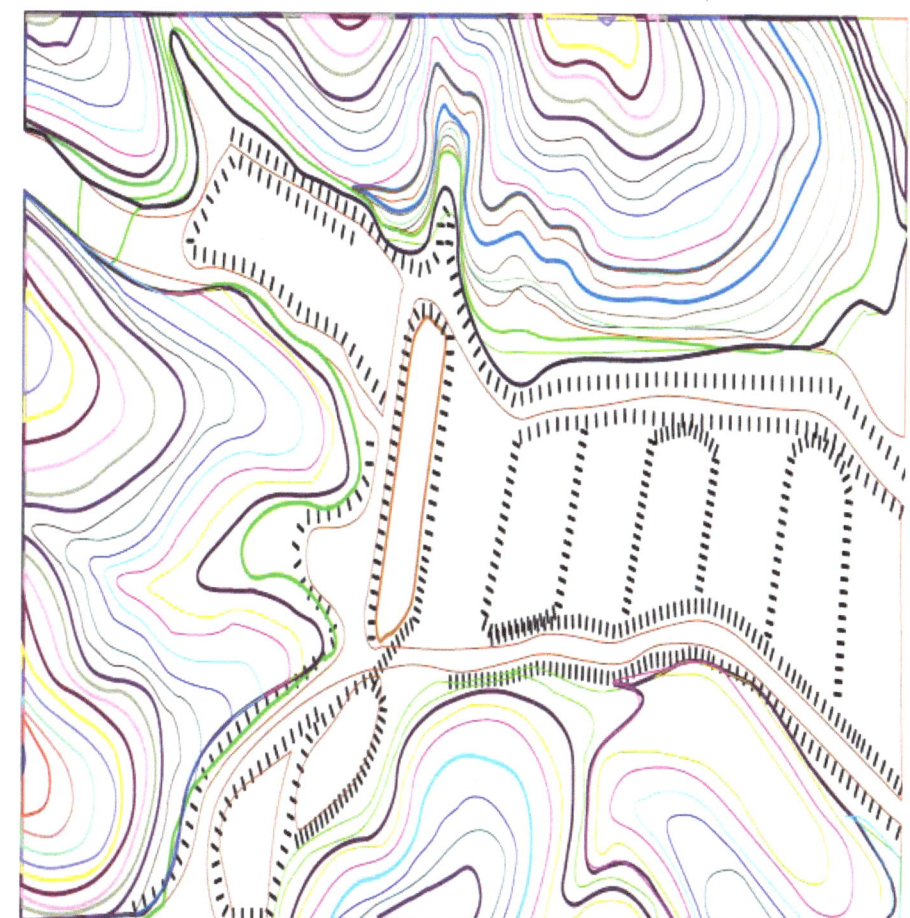

Mini-Kiln
Amiko Matsuo

Mini-Kiln highlights the ironies of digitally fabricating a micro-version of a noborigama, a massive Japanese climbing kiln that fills the space left in a hillside by the removal of materials for its construction.

The portable, replicable, and "unnatural" miniature raises questions about technology, material, and our transitional moment in ceramic history. The translucent walls shed light on the kiln's dark interior, making visible the interiority of the transformative process.

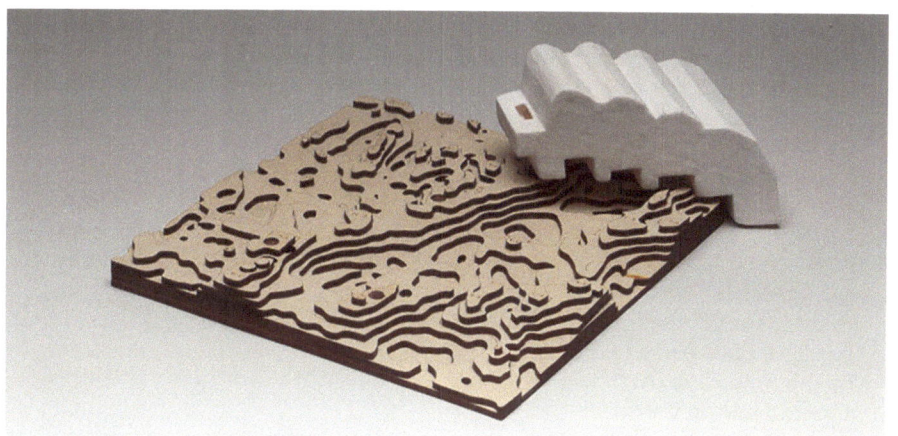

vibrantlands.org

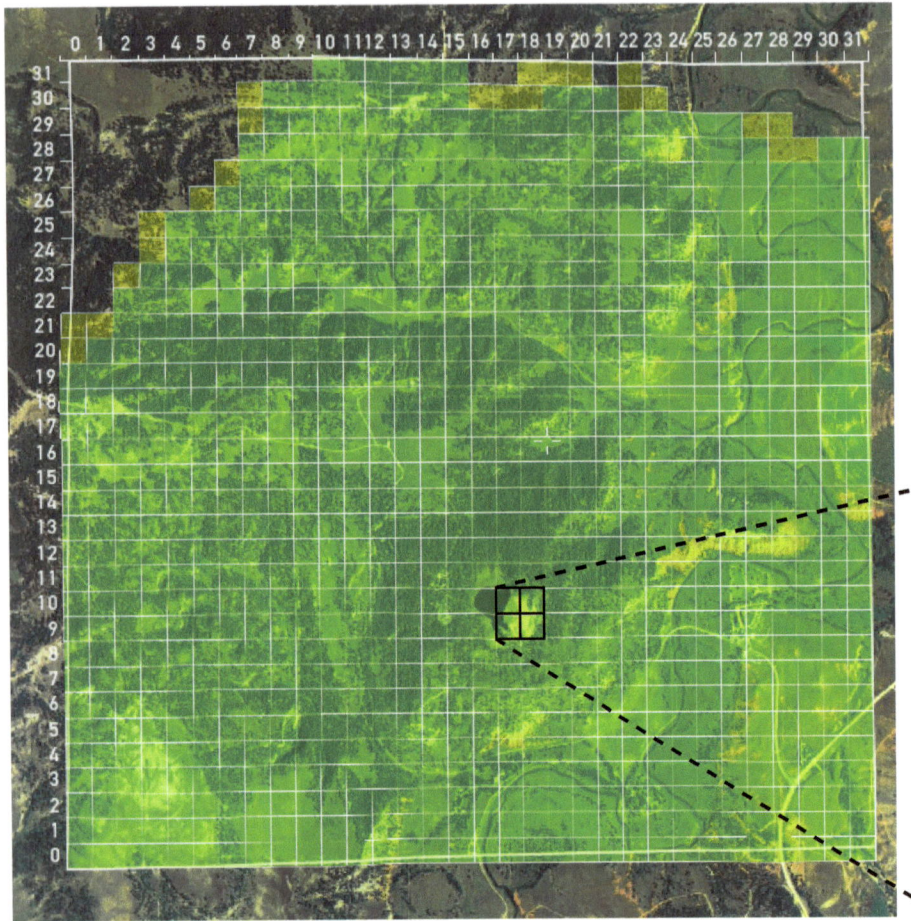

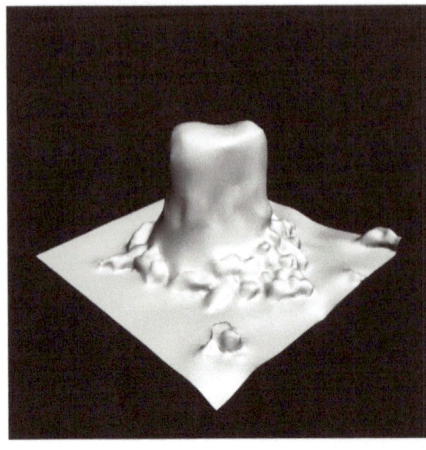

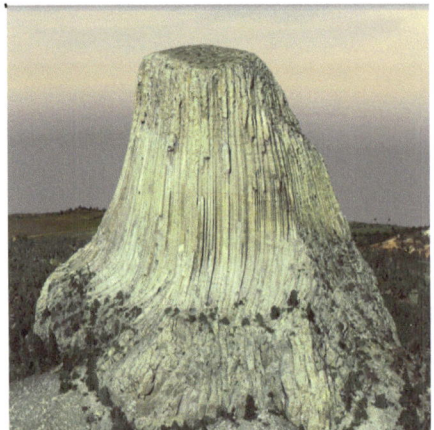

Map of Woolpert Labs model

Woolpert Labs model rendering

Nina was counting on sourcing the model of Devils Tower from the web. There were numerous models available, but not all models are created equal. In the upper right is one that we found on line. It clearly doesn't capture the beauty of the mountain, and both we and Nina quickly rejected it.

Another model was more promising. Woolpert Labs had a beautiful model, complete with texture and lighting, depicted below the first model, and in the map above. Fortunately, the

guys at Woolpert were willing to share their model, if only they could figure out how to export it to us. When they finally did, it came it at 11.5 gigabytes of data, including 3.5 gigabytes of geometry and 8 gigabytes of textures.

We finally got them to narrow this down to the four quadrants (out of 961 originally sent) highlighted in the map at rows 10-11 and columns 17-18. However, each of these quadrants still overwhelmed Wikitude.

Many hours have gone into trying to

pare this enormous model down to something you can see in this book.

The fun thing about this particular artwork is that what you see when you first look at it is the best we could do at press time.

Over time, this model will improve. Artist Reilly Donovan has stepped in to help us compress it and re-map the textures to work with the technology. Check back next week or next month, and the model will have come closer to Nina's original vision.

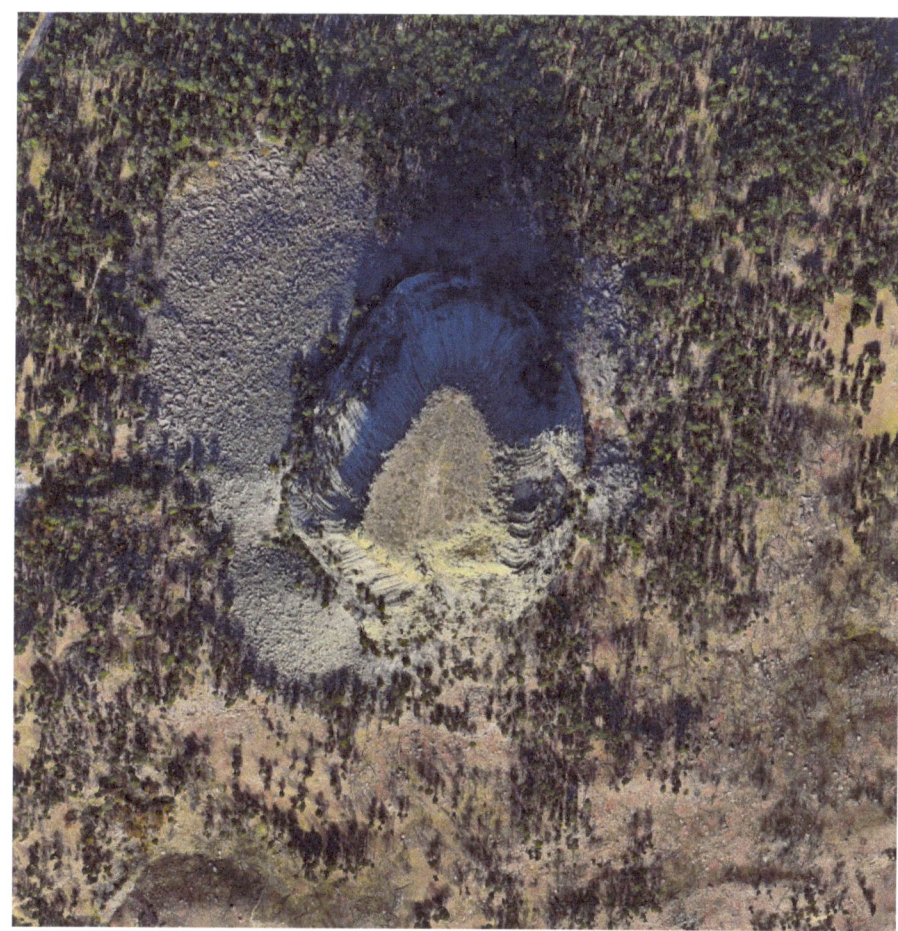

Devils Tower
Nina McGowan

Not only did 'Close Encounters' deal with future technologies, it documented the construction of Devils Tower across a number of physical platforms. In the narrative it enters the hero Roys mind as a telepathically transmitted image sent from a higher intelligence, that so besieged him he was moved to build its form – firstly in his mashed potatoes at the dinner table, (then in grander scale his living room) but its not until he sees its likeness on the TV, does he realise that it in fact 'exists'.

The human psyche, through stories and legends alone, is pretty indelibly scored with the idea of mountain top ascensions accompanying the possible deliverance of messages from higher intelligences that either reside above the clouds or condescend to make contact where are found pinnacles of spiritual experience.

Devils Tower is held as a sacred place by Native Americans, whose myth describes 7 sisters, who, being chased by bears, took to hiding upon a stony area, where they prayed to the Great Spirit who took pity on them and raised up their platform higher than the bears reach – this is how the 'tower' came to be, however, the bears continued to climb, and the Great Spirt lifted the sisters to the skies for safety where they became the constellation Pleiades. This star system is considered by many early civilisations to be the origin of all life.

In fact, when we hold a mountain made of light in the palm of our hands and occupy the space belonging to Pleiades, it is us who become the gods.

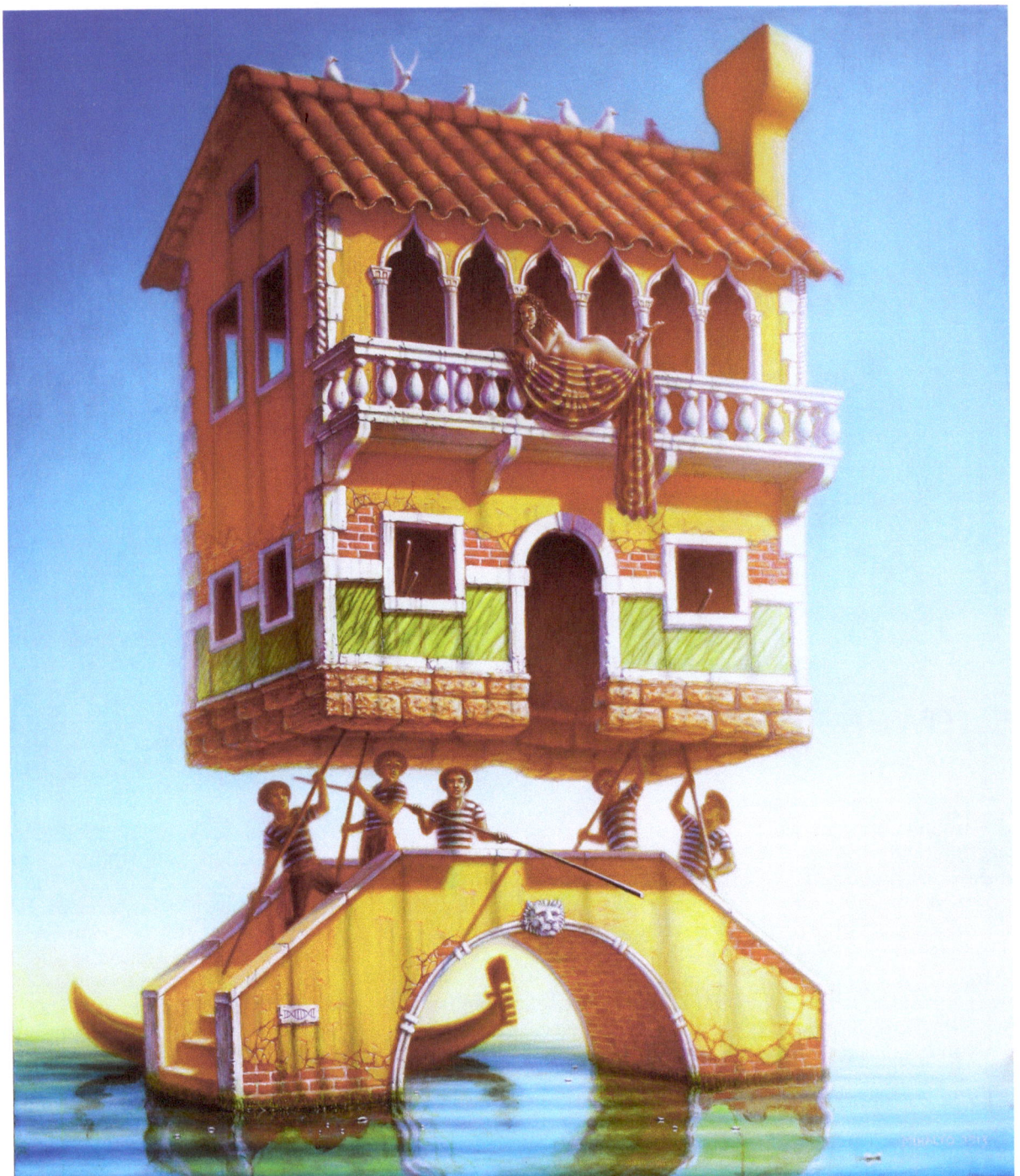

"Suitors"
oil on canvas
2013
75.5" X 65"

Jeff Mihalyo

Pop Up (AR)t

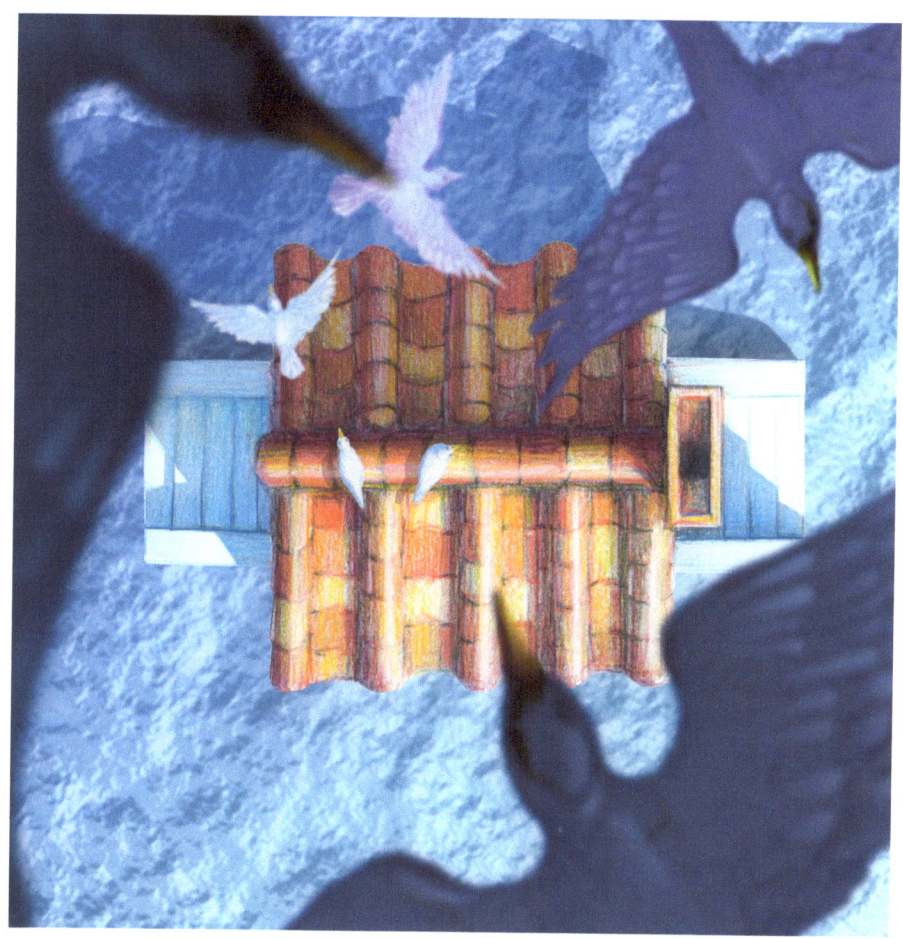

Suitors
Jeff Mihalyo

In his art, Jeff Mihalyo discusses world and philosophical issues through a multifaceted system of symbolic and narrative compositions.

Each painting emphasizes a need for balance in order to explore the complexity of the theme. He conveys the need for balance through a poetic arrangement of his subjects and by presenting multiple viewpoints of an issue within the painting's narrative.

This multi-dimensional approach to the portrayal of a "vision" allows each image to behave as an open-ended statement.

The setting and characters of each picture can appeal to the viewer's psychology, inviting one to develop questions about what is depicted and ultimately draw one's own conclusions about the meaning of the work.

The suggested narrative and viewer interpretation is key to the interplay between the artist and his audience. self-guided discovery of the artwork.

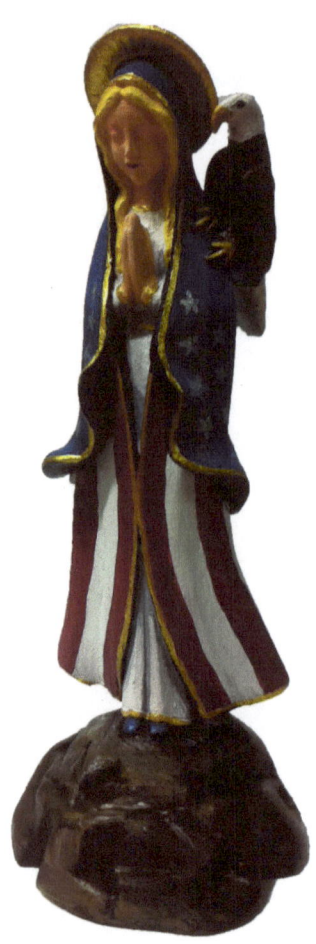

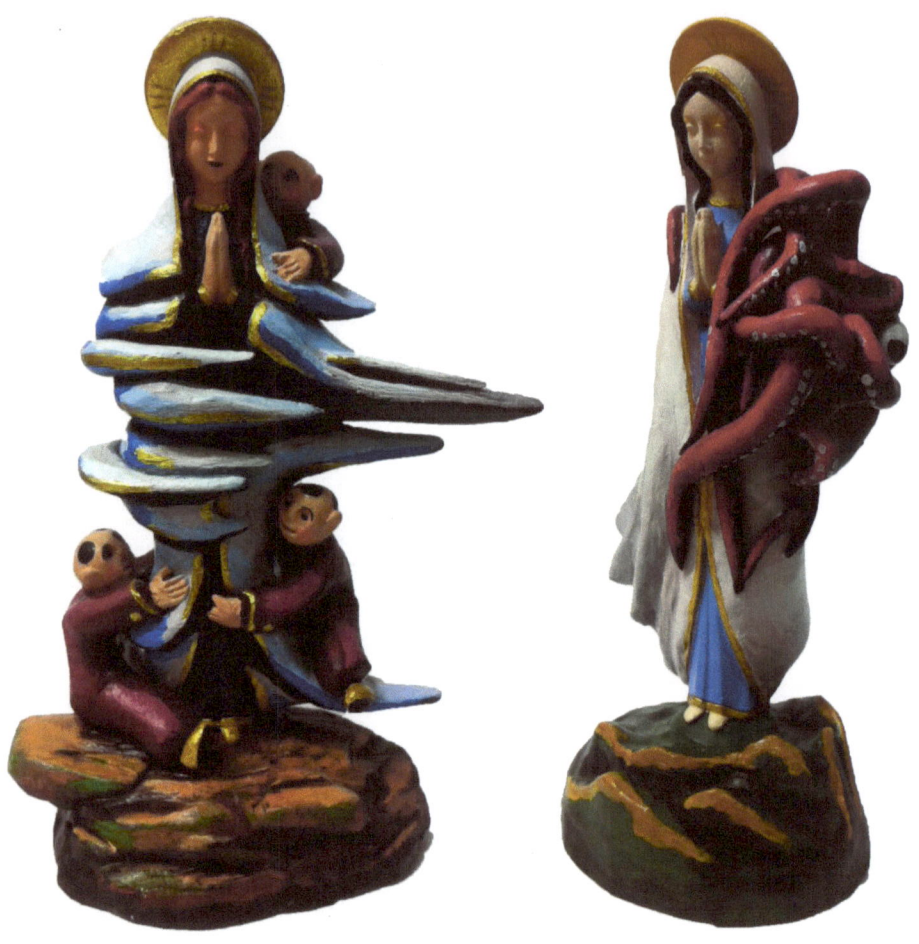

Based on American iconography

Based on Buddhism

Based on a Japanese print

This is a collection of modified Virgin Mary statues. It is an exploration of what could be done to religious imagery, and how we modify such icons to fit our own personal narratives.

We make our own saviors, we define our own gods. In many ways, we all have a personal relationship with Jesus, only his name is not necessarily Jesus, but we hope that someday, he will save us from our dreary lives.

In many of my previous shows, because I currently work in South Korea, I had to hire actors to pretend to be me as the artist. These shows are often built around the fake persona and attendees know that it is indeed an actor walking around during the opening. A show by Niklas Bergman, for example, was built around this artist who created action figures and was releasing them to the public. Having a show this way not only allowed me to work and exhibit at two places at the same

time, but it also gave me creative freedom to explore and make things I normally wouldn't make.

I believe the play between the small visual diaries and the act of exhibiting art, along with the creation of a fake artist, explores the very nature of what the artist is. It examines how artists share their message, how they value their privacy, and how they as an individual affect the art outside of the creation process.

Joseph Reyes

Transformer
Virgin Mary
Joseph Reyes

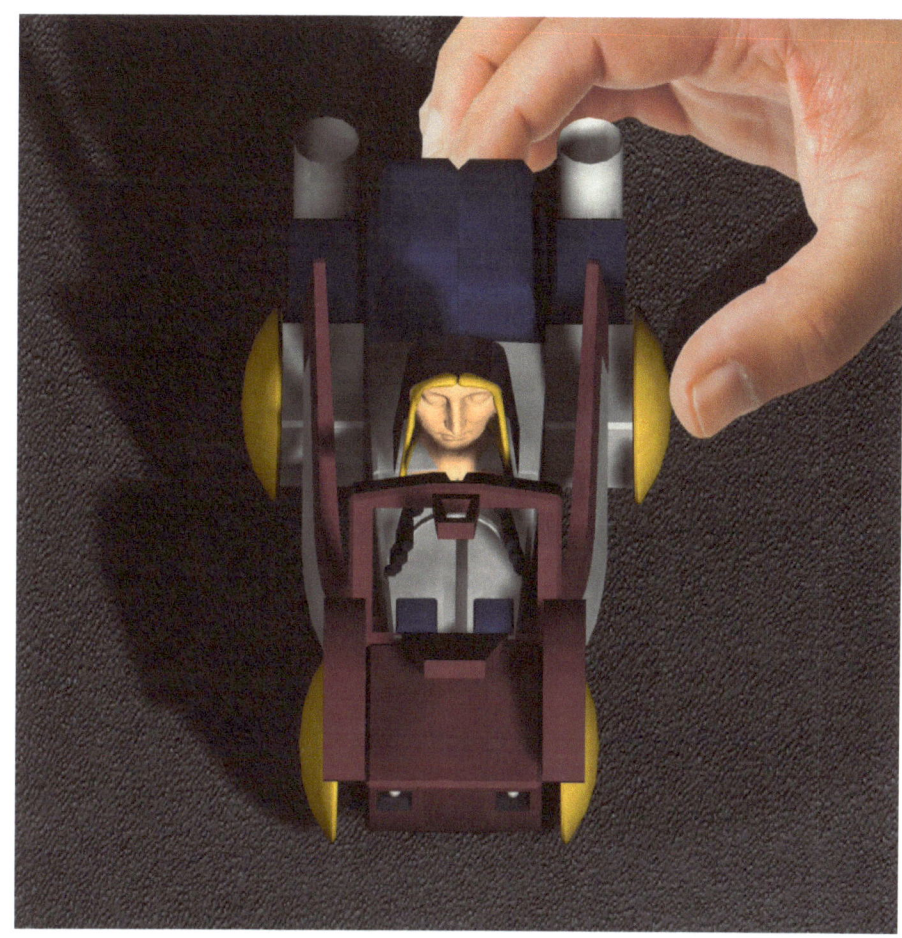

I'm a Canadian currently living and working in South Korea. My medium is mainly pen and ink, but I occasionally make small sculptures.

My drawings are created using text and images that express feelings ranging from isolation, anxiety, and most recently, the longing to be back home. The small text and the limitations of the average person's vision and patience allows me to be honest about many issues since many would not care to study most of the text.

I also create sculptures as ready-made products. My "Action Figure Expo" featured small sculptures of everyday people, which is a more lighthearted way of critiquing my environment.

In this case, the sculptures are about personal salvation be it religious or not, but they are dealt with in a lighthearted manner.

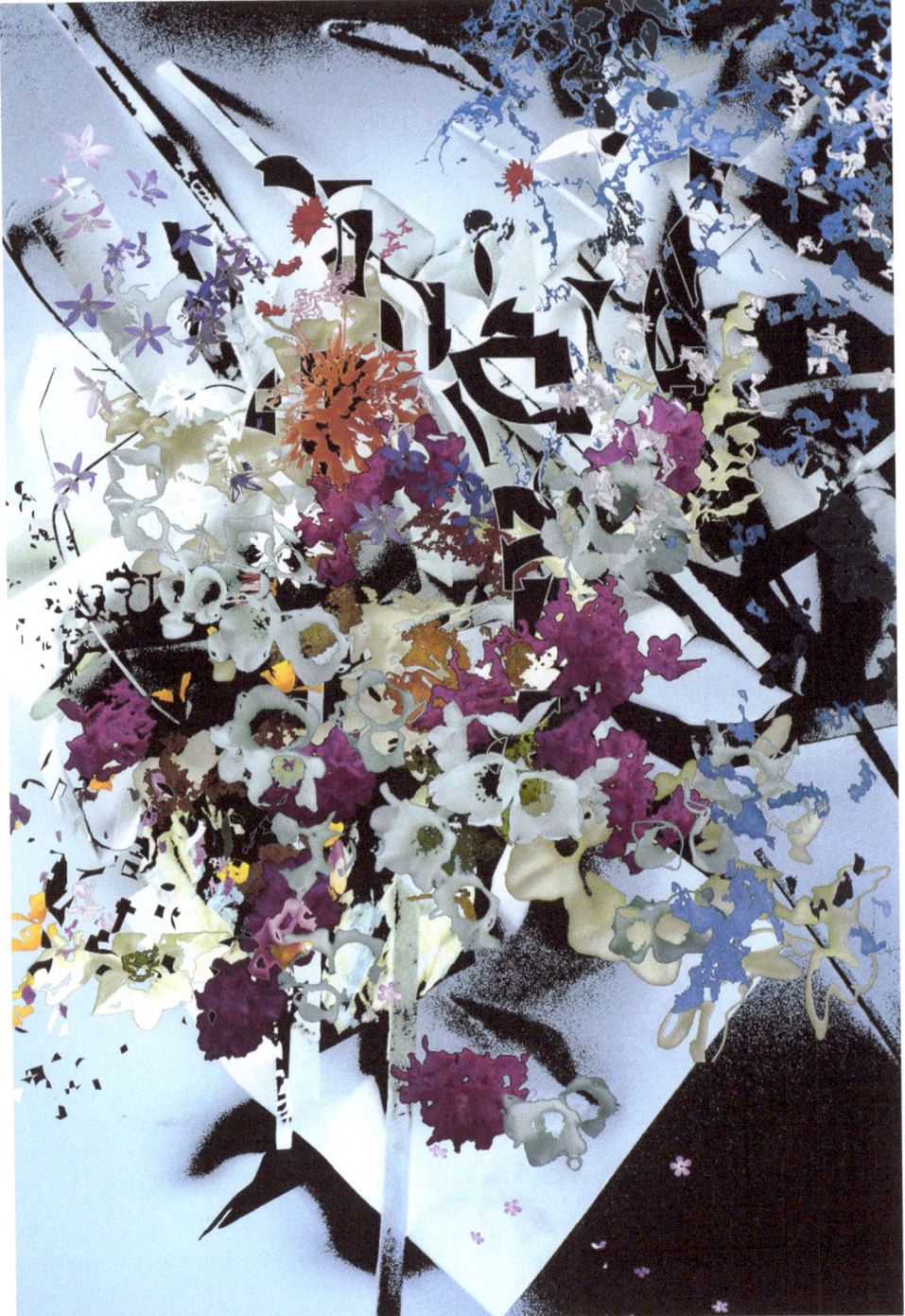

Between Beauty & Chaos
Pigmented print with watercolor &
collage, 32"w x 48"h, 2016

Stephen Rock

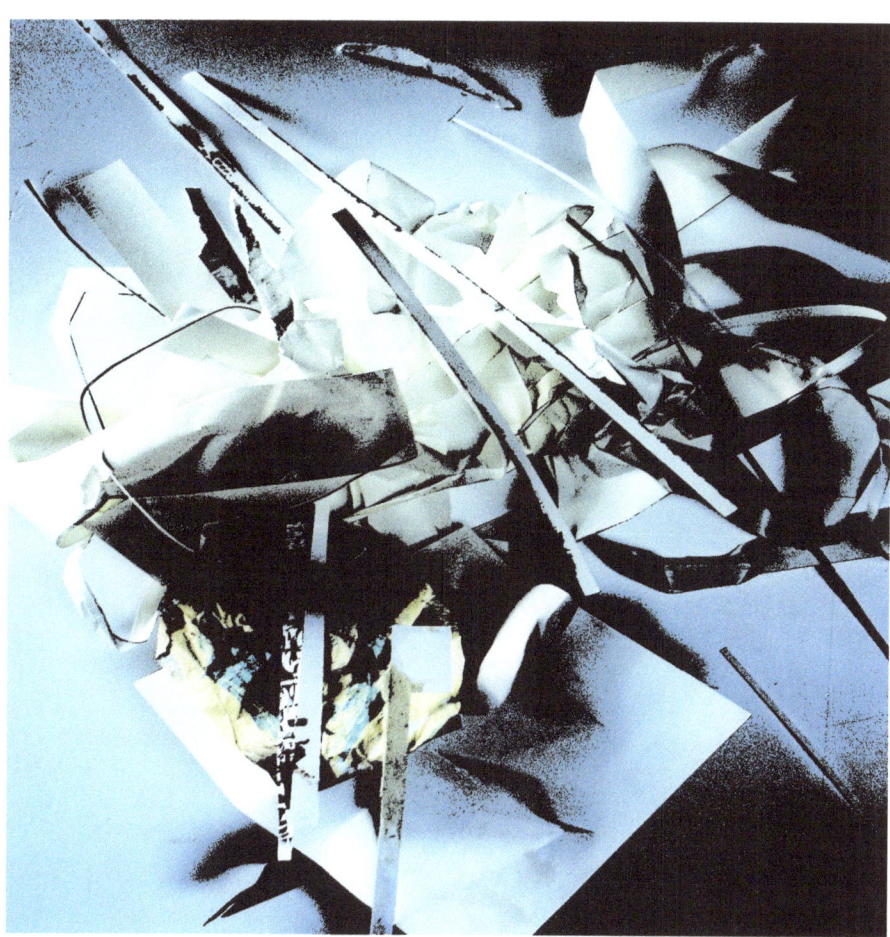

Between
Beauty & Chaos
Stephen Rock

My current work explores our relationship with how we coexist and communicate in the evolving digital community. The images are influenced by an urban aesthetic, a mash-up of cultures and conversation, a style that consumes and reconfigures itself into a new language for the hyphenated, abbreviated, multi-lingual world. I create my images by dissecting text sampled from media newsfeeds, combining it with collaged material, photographs and digitally manipulated elements then output as large format pigmented ink prints in my studio and often add mixed media to the surface as a final touch.

Stephen Rock deconstructs the experiences of life and reconfigures the remnants to create work in a variety of mediums. His recent work has included large and small reclaimed material sculptures, innovative digital works, paintings and conceptual installations.

Rock has been showing original artwork in a variety of mediums for over 30 years. He has received regional and national recognition and awards for his work and his work is in many private and public collections such as the City of Seattle Portable Works, King County Portable Works Collection and the Bainbridge Island Museum of Art.

His larger installations and sculptures have been selected for exhibit through the Center on Contemporary Art (C.O.C.A.) at Carkeek Park, MADART at Cal Anderson Park in Seattle and at the Anacortes, WA. and La Conner, WA Sculpture Festivals.

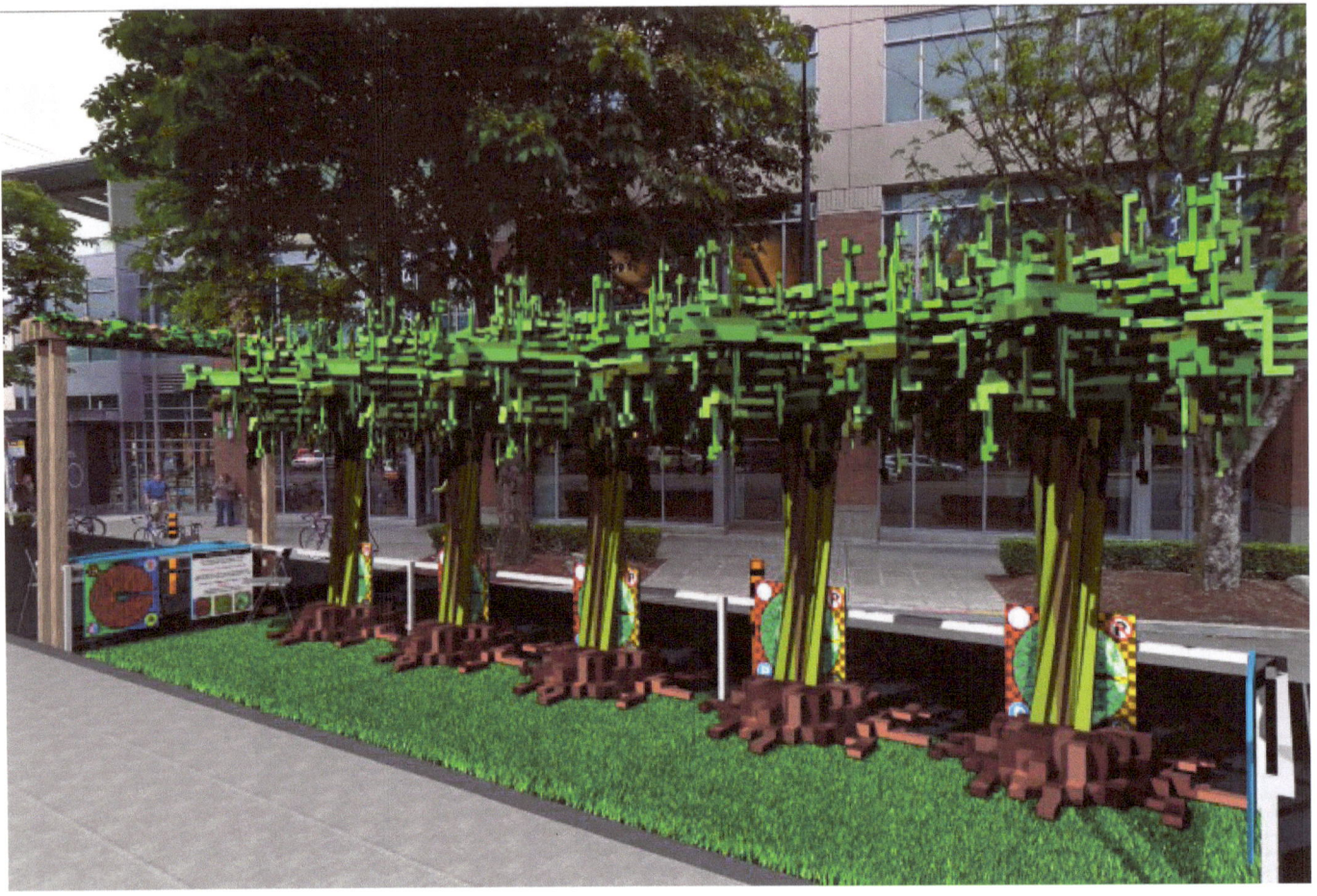

Center on Contemporary Art's p(AR)king Day project celebrates the park that could have been by constructing this Augmented Reality p(AR)k, covering the ground with virtual grass, planting virtual trees by Casey Scalf (www.sensebellum.com) on the street, and providing virtual shade with a virtual ivy-covered trellis.

You are standing on the site of what would have been the Seattle Commons, had Seattle Times columnist John Hinterberger gotten his way.

Hinterberger proposed creating a large green space like New Yorks' Central Park from Westlake Park to South Lake Union, and Microsoft co-founder Paul Allen donated $20m to buy property to make it happen. Along the way the plan evolved to include mixed-income house, retail, and commercial space along the edges of the park.

The project was scuttled when the public voted it down in 1995 and 1996, clearing way for the development now under way.

In addition to the main tree on display at the p(AR)k, illustrated above and presented as an AR model on the next page, Casey also made a number of smaller trees for us to give away on stickers during the event.

These stickers are reproduced below the main image on the following page, and can be accessed through the Wikitude app by searching for "CoCA Tree" in the Wikitude search bar.

Don't forget to go back to "CoCA Pop-Up (AR)t after viewing these.

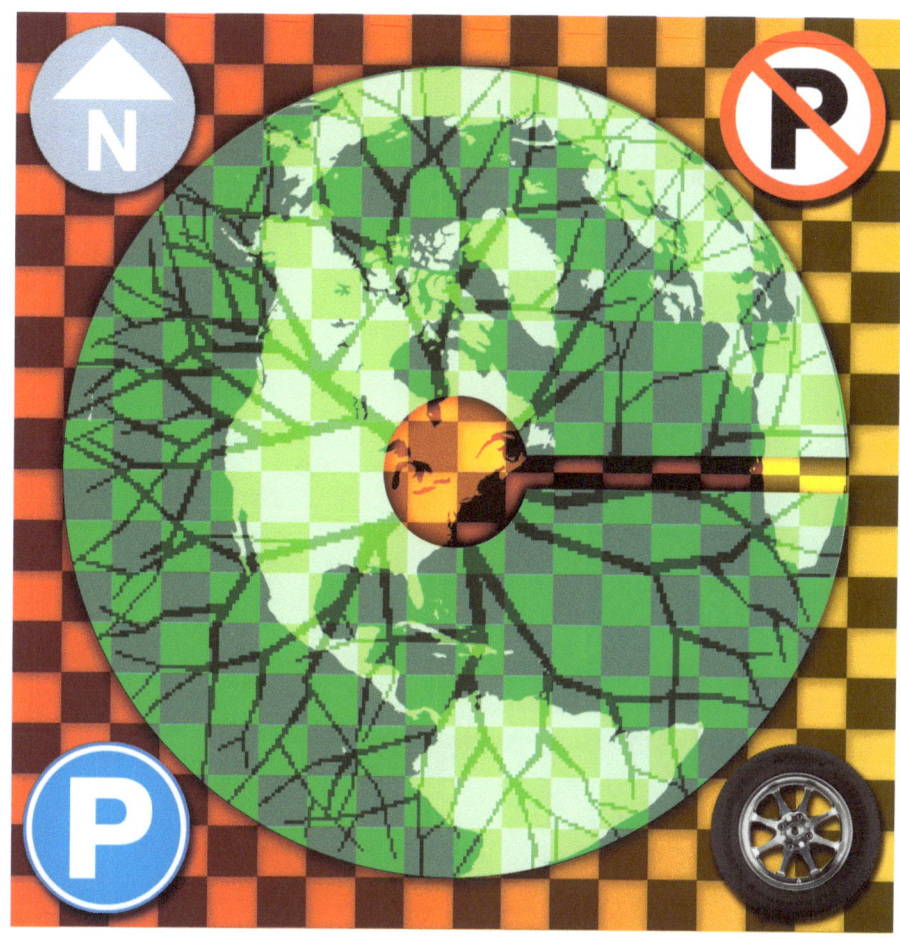

Trees for CoCA p(AR)k
Casey Scalf

Printing courtesy of Rock's Studio

Grow your own tree with this sticker!

in the app,* use code: **cocatree**

www.cocaseattle.org

3D Tree Art: Casey Scalf
www.sensebellum.com
P(AR)King Day Design:
Ray C. Freeman III
www.raycfreemaniii.com

*iOS or Android

Printing courtesy of Rock's Studio

3D Tree Art: Casey Scalf
www.sensebellum.com
P(AR)King Day Design:
Ray C. Freeman III
www.raycfreemaniii.com

www.cocaseattle.org

Grow your own tree with this sticker! in the app,* use code: **cocatree**

*iOS or Android

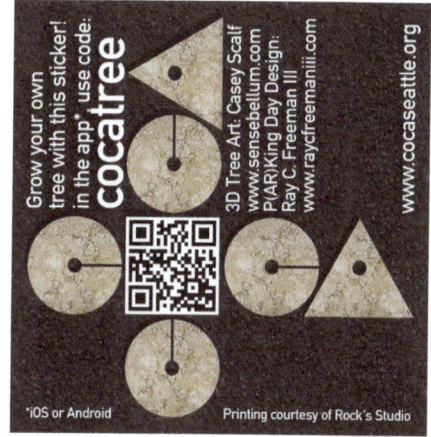

Grow your own tree with this sticker! in the app,* use code: **cocatree**

3D Tree Art: Casey Scalf
www.sensebellum.com
P(AR)King Day Design:
Ray C. Freeman III
www.raycfreemaniii.com

www.cocaseattle.org

*iOS or Android

Printing courtesy of Rock's Studio

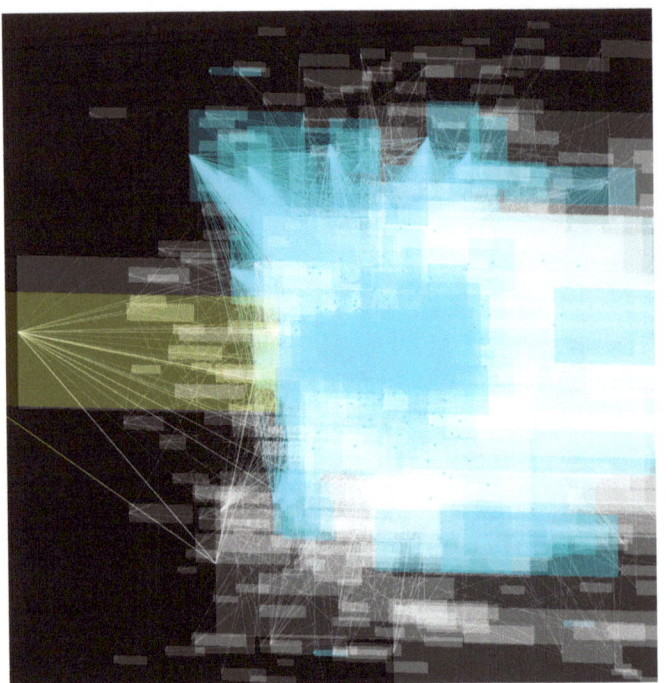
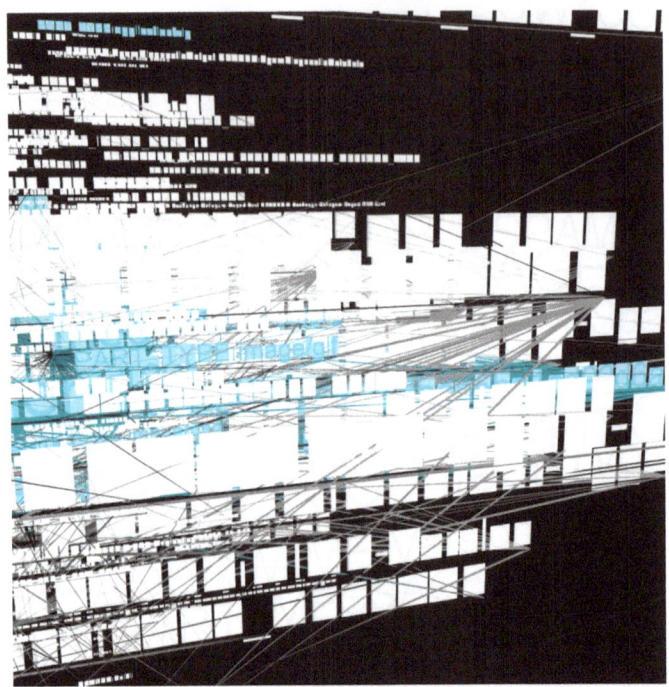
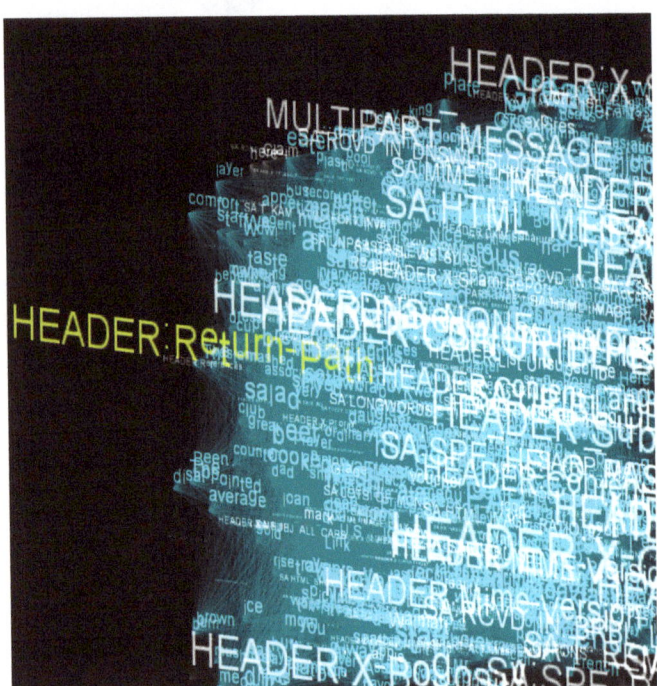
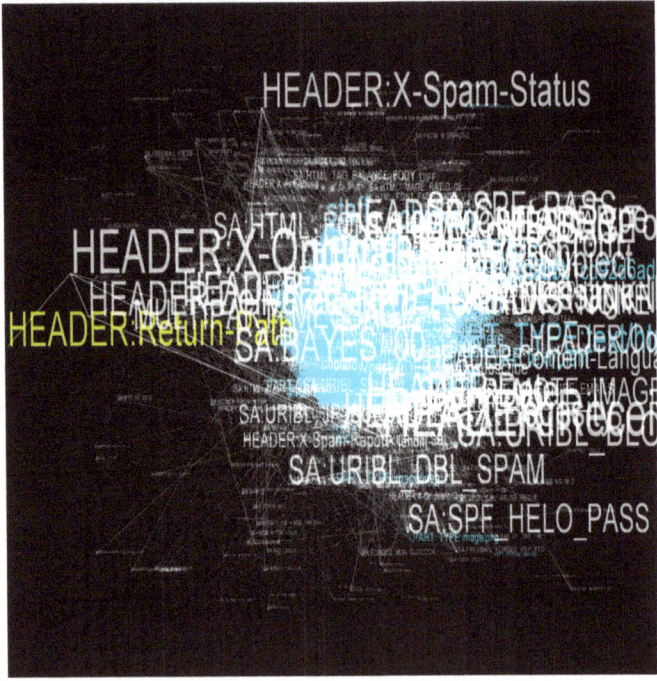

j shagam

Annealed Spam
j shagam

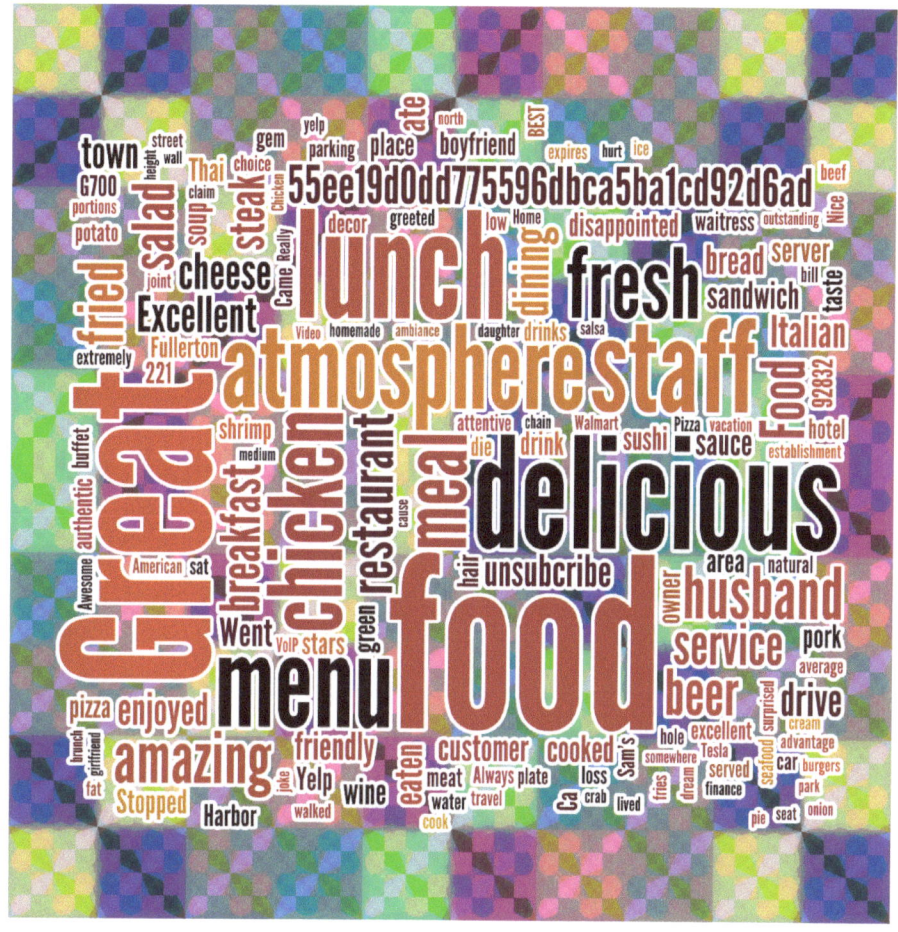

If you have been on the Internet for more than a day or two you have likely received email spam. The term "spam" in this sense comes from the famous Monty Python sketch, in which a restaurant has quite a few dishes all involving Spam™, which the hapless patron does not like. During her protests, vikings appear and dominate the conversation with a song about said potted lunchmeat.

In this work, I apply a statistical analysis to a month's worth of spam messages, looking at both the message structure and the content, and use the relationships between adjacent words to build a 3D object in which the words attempt to arrange themselves based on their frequency and common neighbors. I custom-built the software for this work.

As a software engineer and graphics researcher I am passionate about finding means of making data more tangible and visible to people. I also want to show the beauty of everyday things, while making them both more abstract and more concrete.

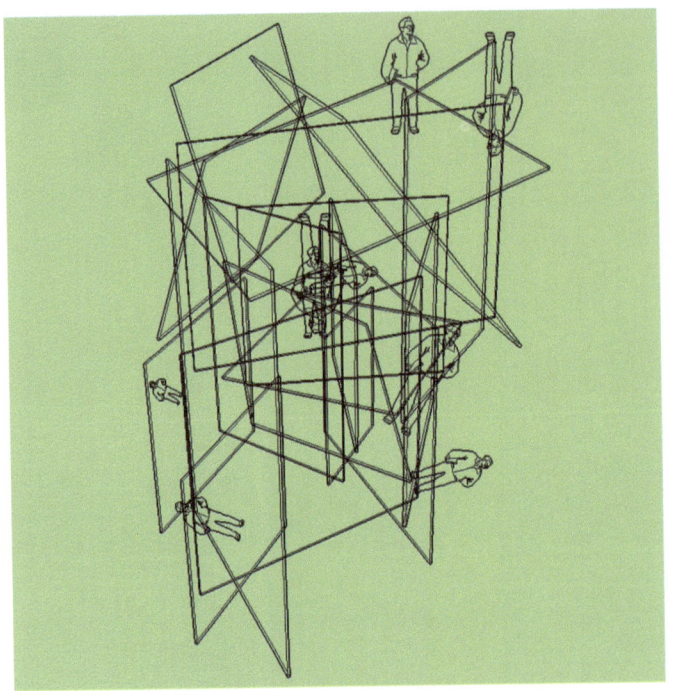
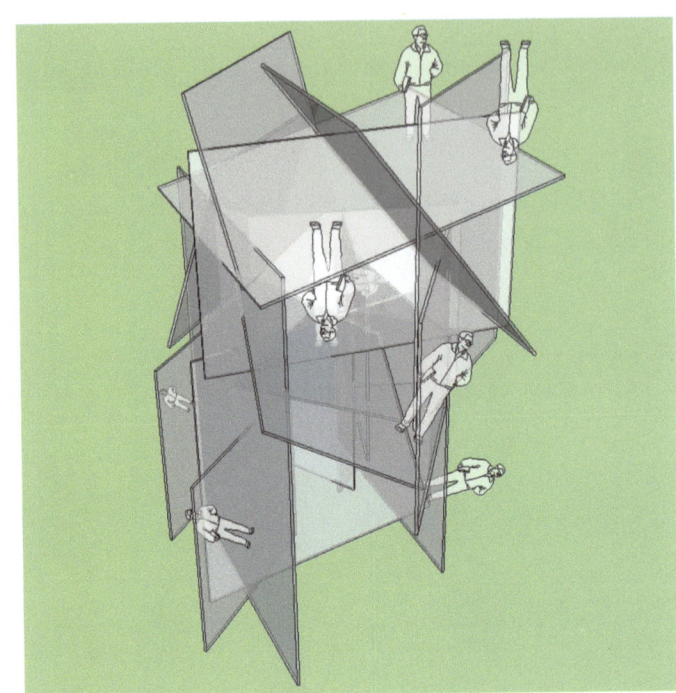
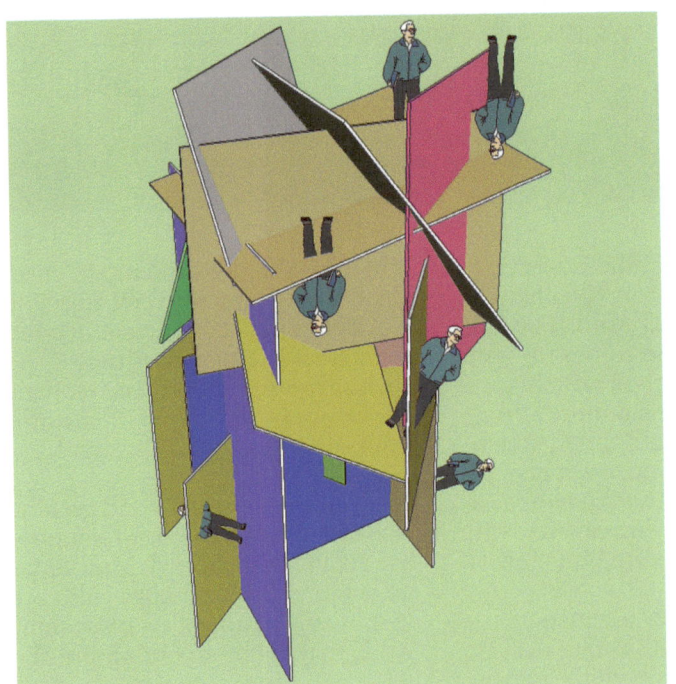
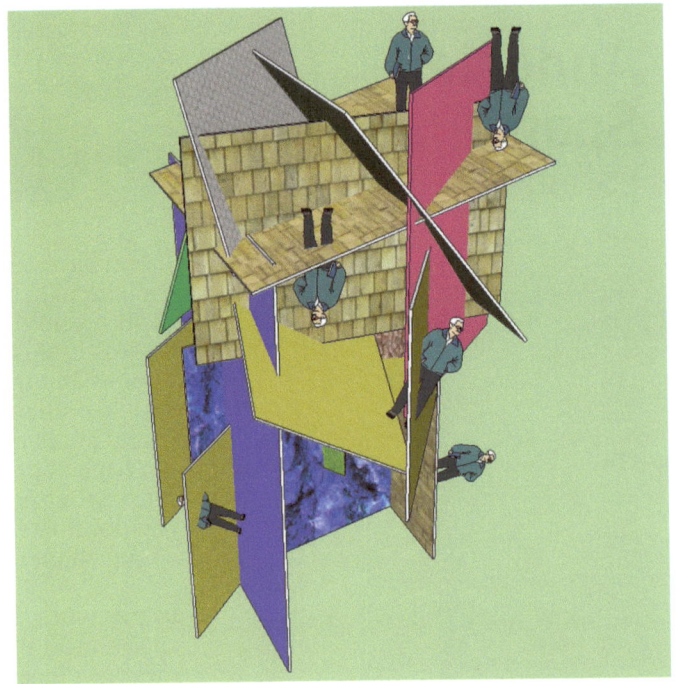

BK Tran

Pop Up (AR)t

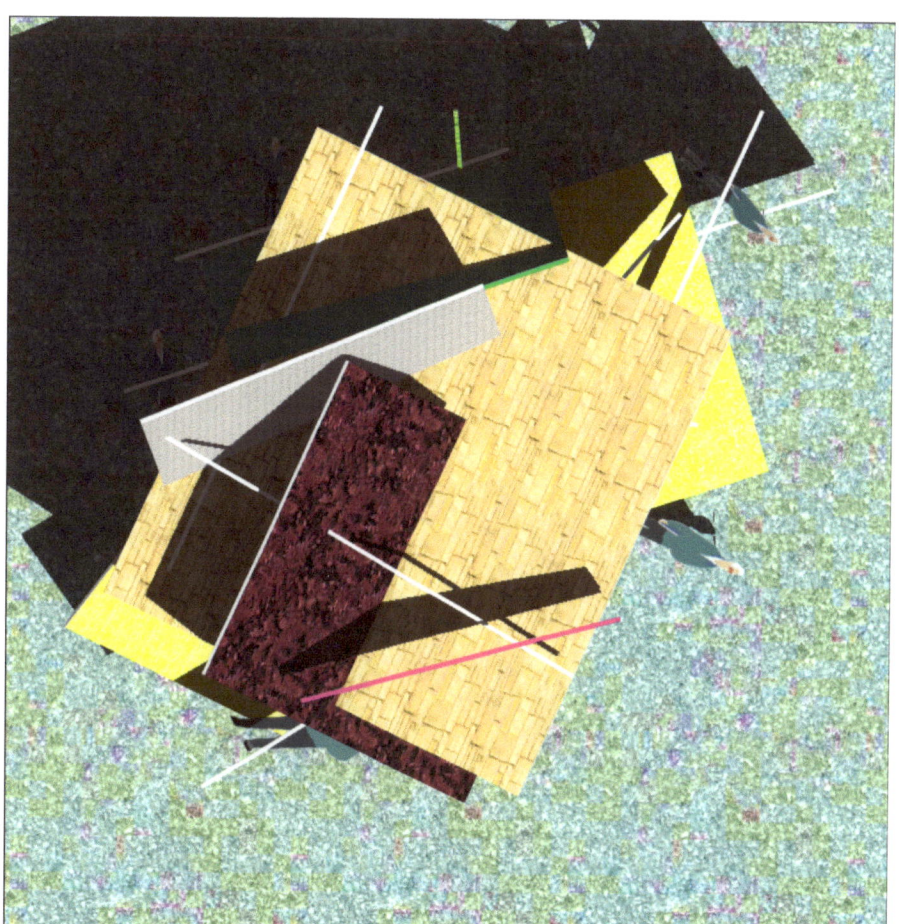

House of Cards
BK Tran

I'm drawn to this project because I have been experimenting with Google SketchUp for a few years and feel as though this would be a good opportunity to see a design turned into 3D.

After stumbling upon the CoCA Pop-up Book project, I quickly came up with a design consisting of intersecting planes that will be built up to create a tall, free-standing structure. Each plane will have an image on both sides and the images will have been taken from the building materials list in the SketchUp program. It

will feel as though I have taken my paintings on canvas and built them up into something much like a house of cards.

Currently I am making art out of discarded materials like electronic parts, wood, plastics, bicycle parts, and so on. I like working with different materials, and like the look of materials in their raw disembodied state. For example, living in West Seattle, I see a lot of new condos and apartments that are presently under construction and I find that I cannot

help but look at these construction sites and get ideas for my art projects. To me, it is far more interesting to look at homes in their unfinished states than it is to see them once they are complete and livable. I feel like this observation is at the root of the idea for my submission.

Beside making art in more traditional ways I have been doing a lot of digital artwork these days.. When working digitally, I can have as many projects as I want and scale them to be just as large as I like.

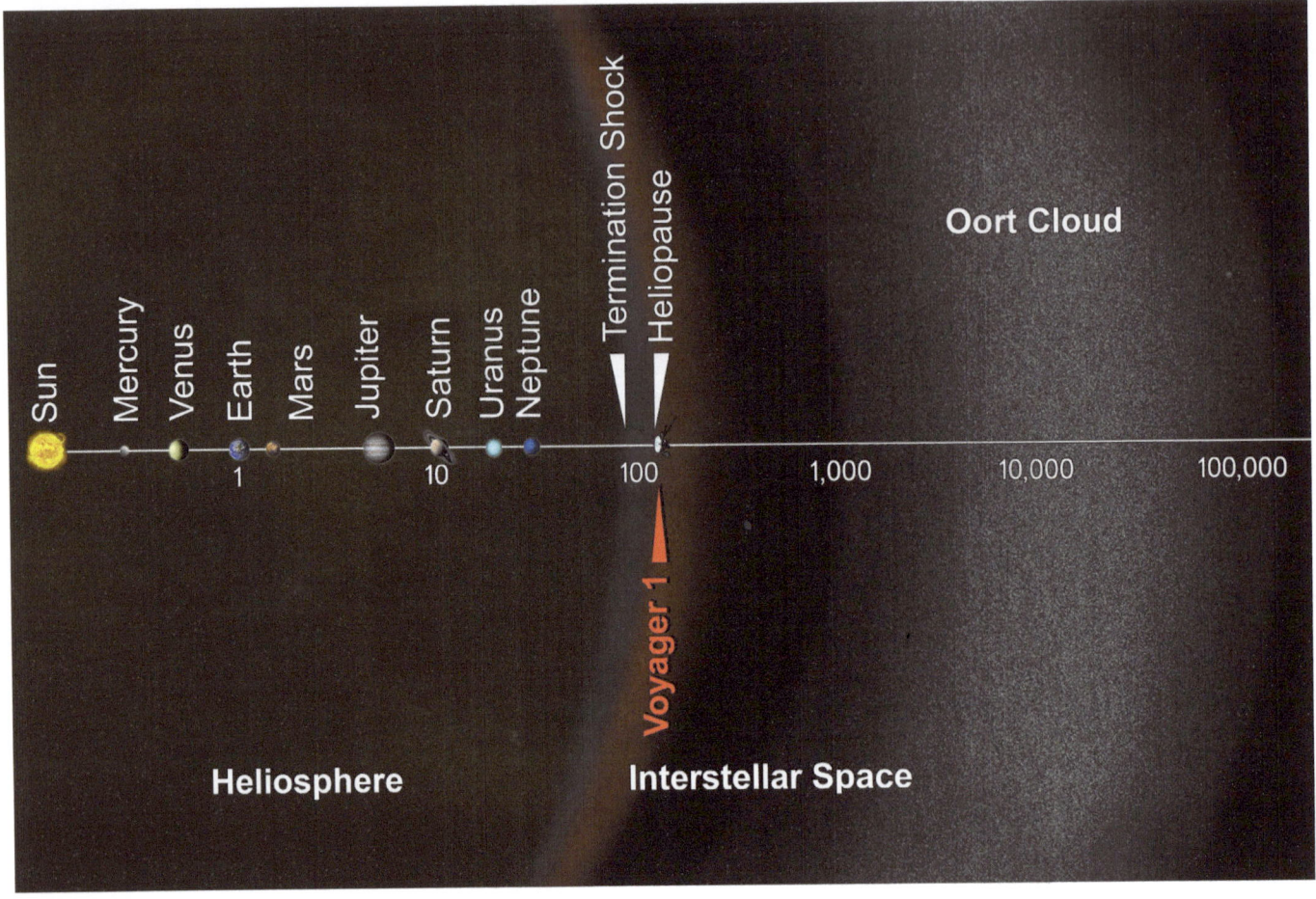

NASA / JPL-Caltech image: Voyager 1 Goes Interstellar

This artist's concept puts solar system distances in perspective. The scale bar is in astronomical units, with each set distance beyond 1 AU representing 10 times the previous distance. One AU is the distance from the sun to the Earth, which is about 93 million miles or 150 million kilometers. Neptune, the most distant planet from the sun, is about 30 AU.

Informally, the term "solar system" is often used to mean the space out to the last planet. Scientific consensus, however, says the solar system goes out to the Oort Cloud, the source of the comets that swing by our sun on long time scales. Beyond the outer edge of the Oort Cloud, the gravity of other stars begins to dominate that of the sun.

The inner edge of the main part of the Oort Cloud could be as close as 1,000 AU from our sun. The outer edge is estimated to be around 100,000 AU.

NASA's Voyager 1, humankind's most distant spacecraft, is around 125 AU. Scientists believe it entered interstellar space, or the space between stars, on Aug. 25, 2012. Much of interstellar space is actually inside our solar system. It will take about 300 years for Voyager 1 to reach the inner edge of the Oort Cloud and possibly about 30,000 years to fly beyond it.

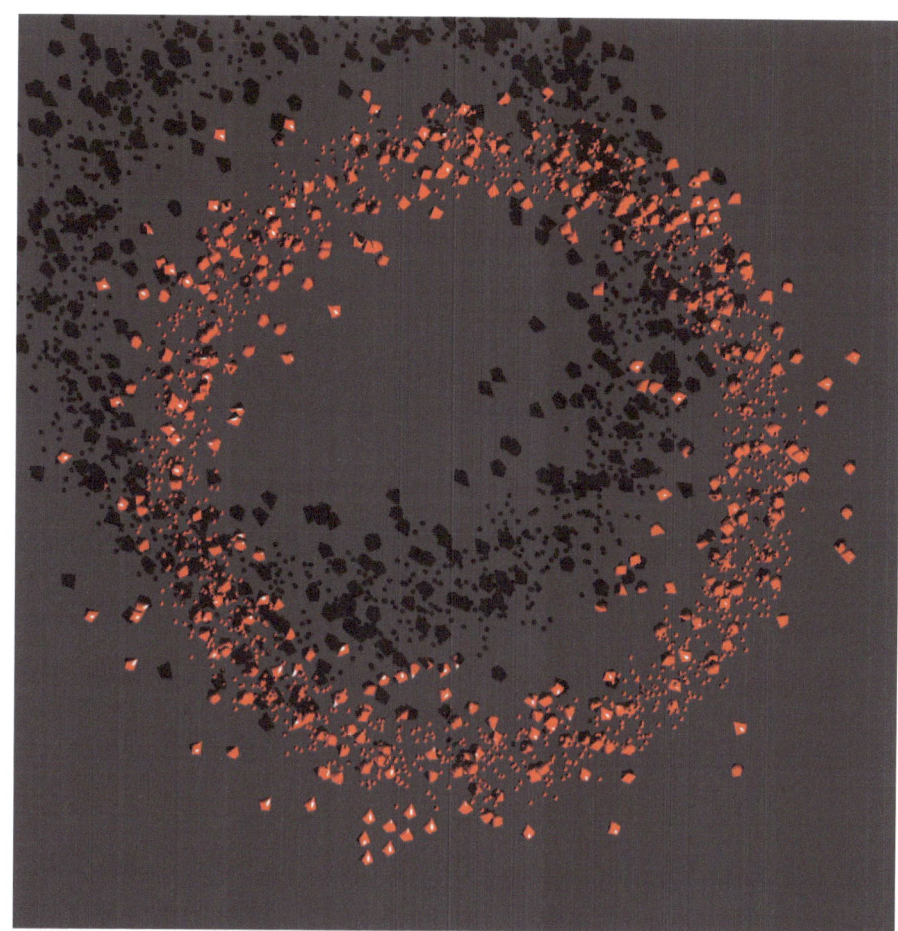

Oort Cloud
Bradley Tsalyuk

Bradley Tsalyuk was born in Los Angeles, CA. He graduated from the School of the Museum of Fine Arts-Boston. He has shown nationally at many artist run spaces. His work has been featured as part of duo and group shows at In The Pines, Howard Art Project, Paragraph Gallery, The San Diego Art Institute, and The New Art Center. He has contributed to the Emergency Index, an annual catalogue of international performance art work. Bradley Tsalyuk currently lives and works in San Diego, CA.

My practice is led by insatiable curiosity, enthusiastic collecting, and research that has evolved as I've continued making work. I often agitate my ideas through a variety of mediums, like a taste test in search of a sublime formula. I'm captivated by facets of contemporary culture that create languages for themselves, speak to history, and generate materials to be appropriated.

My work often focuses on the (un)attainability of knowledge. My research often skims the surface of many subjects, failing to provide any concrete understanding of the depths of specific topics. The tangents I follow in my research highlight the limits of the idea of "an authority."

I created the series of works based on the Oort Cloud because it represents a region of space that the Voyager 1 probe will be entering in about 300 years. By that time the Voyager 1's scientific instruments will have stopped working. The Voyager 1 probe is the farthest human-made object from Earth.

CoCA Books and Catalogs
Available at http://www.lulu.com/spotlight/cocaseattle

Heaven and Earth
Outdoor Sculpture Exhibition at Carkeek Park

2009 Annual Exhibition
Juried by Jess Nostrand

Across the Divide
Contemporary Art from the Scablands and Beyond

2009 East|West
Emerging Artist Exchange

Kate Vrijmoet
Essential Gestures

Across the Divide II
Art from Big Sky Country

Gideon: Becoming
A Story of Love and Cosmology

Resident Alien
Local Artists from Europe and Beyond

CoCA Parks 2010
Outdoor Sculpture Exhibitions

2010 Annual Exhibition: Memory Upgrade
Juried by Juan Alonso

Heaven and Earth III: Cycles of Return
Outdoor Sculpture Exhibition

Limb from Limb
The Arboreal Art of Peppé

(Un)Sanctioned
13 Contemporary Urban Artists

2011 Annual Exhibition
Juried by Gary Hill

Rootbound: Heaven and Earth IV
Outdoor Art Exhibition at Carkeek Park

Across the Divide IV
The New Boondooks

Show Us Yours
2012 CoCA Members' Show

Alive, Dead
28 Artists' Interpretations

2012 Annual Exhibition
Juried by MK Guth

Whitewashed
Joseph Gregory Rossano

CoCA Collision
Past, Present, & Future Members' Show, 2013

Acclimatized: Heaven and Earth 5
Outdoor Art Exhibition at Carkeek Park

Ceci N'est Pas Une Pipe
Flameworking on the Brink of Legalization

Who Are You?
CoCA Members' Show, 2014

2014 Annual Exhibition: PostGlamism
Juried by Mike Sweney

As. Above. So. Below.: Heaven and Earth VI
An Exhibition of Temporary Artwork at Carkeek Park

Change-Seed
Contemporary Art from Hong Kong and Beyond

The Siken Collaboration
Eleven artists respond to Siken's "The War of the Foxes"

Propagation: Heaven and Earth VII
An Exhibition of Temporary Artwork at Carkeek Park

35 Live
2016 CoCA Members' Show and Catalog

Monograph Series:

1. Otherwise This Stone
Poetry by David Francis

2. Field Notes from the Chimalapa Wilderness
David Francis, Oaxaca, 2000-2012

3. The Stars are Made from Love & Beauty
Joe Reno Journals

www.ingramcontent.com/pod-product-compliance
Lightning Source LLC
Chambersburg PA
CBHW050824180526

45159CB00004B/1775